The Hipster Economy

The Hipster Economy

*Taste and authenticity in late
modern capitalism*

Alessandro Gerosa

First published in 2024 by
UCL Press
University College London
Gower Street
London WC1E 6BT

This book is freely available on a Creative Commons CC-BY-NC-ND licence thanks to the kind sponsorship of the libraries participating in the Jisc Open Access Community Framework OpenUP initiative.

Available to download free: www.uclpress.co.uk

Text © Author, 2024

The author has asserted his rights under the Copyright, Designs and Patents Act 1988 to be identified as the author of this work.

A CIP catalogue record for this book is available from The British Library.

Any third-party material in this book is not covered by the book's Creative Commons licence. Details of the copyright ownership and permitted use of third-party material is given in the image (or extract) credit lines. If you would like to reuse any third-party material not covered by the book's Creative Commons licence, you will need to obtain permission directly from the copyright owner.

This book is published under a Creative Commons Attribution-Non-commercial Non-derivative 4.0 International licence (CC BY-NC-ND 4.0), https://creativecommons.org/licenses/by-nc-nd/4.0/. This licence allows you to share, copy, distribute and transmit the work for personal and non- commercial use provided author and publisher attribution is clearly stated. Attribution should include the following information:

Gerosa, A., 2024. *The Hipster Economy: Taste and authenticity in late modern capitalism.* London: UCL Press. https://doi.org/10.14324/111.9781800086067

Further details about Creative Commons licences are available at https://creativecommons.org/licenses/

ISBN: 978-1-80008-608-1 (Hbk.)
ISBN: 978-1-80008-607-4 (Pbk.)
ISBN: 978-1-80008-606-7 (PDF)
ISBN: 978-1-80008-609-8 (epub)
DOI: https://doi.org/10.14324/111.9781800086067

Contents

Acknowledgements	vii
Introduction: contextualising the hipster economy	1
1 A *longue durée* quest towards the meaning of authenticity	17
2 The hip aesthetic regime of consumption	37
3 The renaissance of neo-craft industries	59
4 The neo-craft micro-entrepreneurs	75
5 The hipster economy and the urban space	93
Concluding remarks: the past, present and future of the hipster economy	107
Notes	117
References	121
Index	127

Acknowledgements

I once stumbled upon a comic strip from Jorge Cham, which – overturning the famous moon-landing quote – argued jokingly that each PhD represents 'a giant leap for one person, an insignificant step for humanity'. I found it a compelling reminder during my academic journey. The same can be argued for publishing a book, which according to current estimates happens around 2 million times a year. Nevertheless, I feel enormously privileged to have had the opportunity of authoring a monograph, and I am moved thinking about the number of people met, the bonds tightened and the help received during this long path. This book would not have been possible without all these contributions. I am even more proud of having the opportunity to publish it in Open Access, contributing to a movement to (hopefully) free and disseminate academic knowledge. For this reason, my gratitude goes to Chris Penfold at UCL Press, who has given this monograph an opportunity; to the patient editorial help along the process; and to the anonymous reviewers for their precious feedback and support. My heartfelt thanks to Michela Vignola for lovingly crafting the amazing cover image for the book, enduring and accommodating my comments.

I must thank Adam Arvidsson, the best mentor that a young scholar could have and the main culprit for my decision to (try to) become a sociologist. I am very grateful to Luisa Leonini for the guidance along the doctoral journey at the base of this book, which has been invaluable. I cannot probably fully acknowledge Alessandro Gandini for all the suggestions and support provided and the many discussions on hipsterism and the neo-craft industries, which informed many intuitions contained in this book. Jennifer Smith Maguire has my gratitude for having been exceptionally engaging and supportive with her comments and suggestions on the doctoral thesis, as well as Marianna d'Ovidio and Ivana Pais for their reviews of it. I must also thank Mark Banks for having welcomed me at CAMEo as a visiting scholar and for our dialogues – a formatively extraordinary experience.

I am grateful to all the scholars who provided me with feedback and support during my PhD and writing of this monograph, allowing for the strengthening of its depth and quality, such as Enzo Colombo, Giulia Giorgi, Chris Land, Annalisa Murgia, Richard E. Ocejo, Giovanni Semi, Maria Tartari, Thomas Thurnell-Read and Marta Tonetta. The majority of this book has been written during my new experience at the University of Birmingham, and my thankfulness goes to all the amazing colleagues that I have met there, especially Caroline Moraes and Rohit Varman for the many insightful discussions on craft and capitalism.

My doctoral journey would not have been the same without the extended academic network of colleagues at the NASP, forming an invaluable network of knowledge exchange and mutual aid. In the same way, I am thankful for having met in my early career a group of fantastic scholars – from whom I have learned a lot and received much support – such as Alberto, Alessandro, Carolina, Davide, Elanor, Guido, Ilir, Lucia, Massimo, Maitrayee, Silvia, Silvia and Vincenzo (to mention only some).

A special mention goes to Fabio, a true adjunct sociology mentor – as well as a true and astonishingly patient friend – who bears great responsibility for my choice to undertake the academic path. Finally, to the ones that made all of this possible: my family and my friends. You supported me, enriched my life and gave me continuous inspiration, making me the person that I am today. Thank you all.

'Know thyself' was written over the portal of the antique world. Over the portal of the new world, 'Be thyself' shall be written.

          Oscar Wilde, *The Soul of Man under Socialism*

In handicrafts and manufacture, the workman makes use of a tool. In the factory, the machine makes use of him.

                Karl Marx, *Das Kapital*

Introduction: contextualising the hipster economy

When I was at the very beginning of my PhD, I had quite clear ideas about my research project. I wanted to study the new trajectories of development of late modern capitalism.[1] And I intended to accomplish this task by analysing the dynamics at the forefront of the economy: start-ups and their billionaire gurus, digital platforms, and the financialisation of the economy. Milan, the economic and financial capital of Italy, seemed like the perfect place to conduct my research. Thus, during my first year, I started to review the many policies introduced by the local government to support new entrepreneurial projects. It was then that I noticed something puzzling: the vocabulary and buzzwords used by these policies were those typical of the start-up economy, but their aim was funding small entrepreneurial projects, mostly in the food and beverage sector. I was looking for disruptive digital innovations, and I found *platanos fritos*.[2] As I noticed this pattern repeating again and again, I started to pay closer attention, and shortly thereafter I ended up changing my empirical case study quite radically. It shifted away from digital platforms and became about gourmet food trucks and cocktail bars, abandoning high-tech start-uppers craving for venture capital in favour of micro-entrepreneurs[3] opening bricks-and-mortar shops. I remember being thrilled but also worried by a simple and candid concern: 'I wanted to study the forefront of contemporary capitalism; will I end up being the sociologist of gourmet burgers instead?' My mentor reassured me that my empirical case study would prove to be an equally valid path to reach the same goal. He was right, an unpleasant but constant feature of supervisors during doctoral journeys.

Indeed, this book – which gathers the outcome of some years of reflections following my PhD research – will argue that the study of professions as humble and apparently marginal as independent craft brewers, food truck vendors and cocktail bartenders, can shed some light on significant social and economic features of late modern capitalism, particularly in the field of consumption. To understand why, it is probably best to start by juxtaposing three brief ethnographic vignettes from different sources:

> Kevin wears a denim apron with a pin reciting 'antifascist bartender' over a plain black shirt. He is very proud of his liquor cellar, with bottles from all around the world, many of them bought during trips abroad. During our interview, when I ask him how his cocktails are born, he tells me that 'The cocktail often starts from a particular element. I happen to go to my trusted herbalist and ask him "What do you recommend this time?" Last time, for example, he recommended a smoked black Chinese tea, and from there the others [from the bar] and I started to elaborate a new cocktail.' He provides another example: 'We have this cocktail called "spritz de matt" ["spritz of fools", in Milanese dialect], which is quite an elaborate drink and has nothing to do with the actual spritz with prosecco. It is a declination of typical aperitif liquors in another form, with Select, Biancosarti and a little vodka, it is what is called a Long Island iced tea with a top of tonic water instead of coke.'
>
> (Personal ethnographic notes, interview with Kevin, translation by the author)

> Craft cocktail bars resemble taste cathedrals, sacred places for making and consuming cocktails. The seriousness of practising mixology structures the fun of public drinking. Owners design them [bars, ed.] by making cocktails and providing a specific drinking experience in mind . . . One night I take a seat at the bar and order a Red Baron off the menu, a stirred cocktail with Aviation Gin, Carpano Antica vermouth, Ramazzotti Amaro, and Maraska Maraschino liqueur. It's a spirit-forward, stirred cocktail, essentially a variation on a Martini. A small group of two young men and a young woman watch Kate, tonight's bartender, make my drink. Wearing a white button-down shirt, an apron over black dress pants, and a vest, her movements are precise as she sets down the mixing glass and precisely measures each ingredient with a jigger.
>
> (Ocejo, 2017, pp. 45–6)

> Rogerio Igarashi Vaz is the owner of 'Bar Trench – Craft cocktails and absinthe'. The bar has a distinctively vintage design and atmosphere, and he wears a very elegant grey waistcoat over a white shirt. Demonstrating a new cocktail to his apprentice, he tells

the idea behind it is to take the original recipe and twist it using purified grapefruit with gin, instead of vodka. When a new client enters, he asks him what he is looking for that evening. The customer answers 'Something light': he then proposes him a Garibaldi, arguing it is a traditional Italian cocktail. After a while, speaking to the camera, he explains that 'In Japan, there is a strong culture of shokunin, that means artisan or a person that is always pursuing to better their craft'.

(Personal notes from watching
MidNight Asia documentary on Netflix)

Kevin, the protagonist of the first vignette, is one of the cocktail barmen or 'bartenders' that I interviewed for my PhD. At the time, he worked at a cocktail bar in Milan, Italy (in the meantime, he has opened his own cocktail bar with some associates). The second vignette is taken from one of the magnific ethnographic accounts illustrated by Richard E. Ocejo (2017) in *Masters of Craft* – one of the major influences on this book. Kate, the worker serving Ocejo, is a bartender at Death & Co., a cocktail bar in New York City, United States. The protagonist of the third vignette is Rogerio Igarashi Vaz, the owner of the Trench bar in Tokyo, Japan. He is one of the protagonists of the first episode of *Midnight Asia*, a documentary available on Netflix exploring the nightlife of Asian megacities. Overall, they work at or own cocktail bars located in three different continents, thousands of kilometres apart from one another. Nevertheless, they share striking resemblances. The bars in which they work are designed with a similar atmosphere. They dress in a similar fashion. More critically, their approach to the profession and the way that cocktails are conceived and prepared may differ by some detail, but they – and their patrons – ultimately wish to produce and consume the same things. They all look for something rooted in tradition but with an innovative twist, which makes it distinctive; something passionately and carefully handcrafted as a unique piece; something assembled from simple, high-quality ingredients. In one word, something *authentic*.

Indeed, writing a book to argue that authenticity has become relevant in contemporary society would today appear akin to writing a book to share with the world that I have just invented the wheel. A great number of authors have already recognised that authenticity has become a fundamental concept in the most disparate disciplines and contexts. Many of them are giants, authorities in their fields, whose analytical and theoretical strength informed my curiosity and inspired the contents of this book. However, as I climbed to stand on their shoulders, I couldn't help thinking that one fundamental 'research puzzle' – as it would be termed in formal academic terms – remained at least partially unanswered: *how* and *why* has authenticity become central in so many different aspects of contemporary society, and in many different sociocultural contexts, too? To deal with such a question would mean to find a common thread, some element explaining the reasons why from New York, to Tokyo, to Milan, experiencing authenticity has become what motivates human labour and makes people's mouths water like few other things. This book argues that the root of the answer lies in the recognition that hipsterism, defined as an aesthetics based on the achievement of an authentic and distinctive experience, represents a dominant paradigm of consumption (at least discursively) in post-Fordist capitalism. Before diving deep into the heart of the book, it appears necessary to specify two premises: what we mean by hipsterism, and what we refer to when talking of post-Fordist capitalism.

Beyond hipsterism as a subculture

I began using the term 'hipster' in my thesis to solve an impasse. Both the entrepreneurs that I was interviewing (gourmet food truck operators, bartenders and restaurateurs) and I were fully aware that, even if indistinguishable from a commodity-related point of view, they belonged to a different economy compared to their 'traditional' counterparts. However, neither they nor I were able to give it a proper definition: usually, they resorted to a definition by opposition. Food truckers told me that they were 'a different job from roach coaches',[4] bartenders told me that their bar was 'different from copy-cat bars',[5] which were instead all similar to each other. After a while, I realised that when I had to explain to external people who the targets of my research were – for instance, when talking to friends or academic colleagues – the easiest way to get my message across was to label them as part of the urban 'hipster economy'. My interlocutor, who had looked at me with a confused stare until that point, usually nodded positively at this reference. However, I knew it represented a shortcut, pragmatically efficient but theoretically problematic: while the hipster label as a buzzword captured very well the aesthetics that distinguished and marked these shops as belonging to a common category, as a label it remained ambiguous and undefinable.

Indeed, in common knowledge, 'hipster' is considered a subculture. In the existing literature, it has been conceptualised as a 'micro-population' (Maly and Varis, 2016), a postmodern mainstream-subculture

(Kinzey, 2012; Schroeder, 2002) or a subculture with countercultural traits (Cronin *et al.*, 2014). What defines something or someone as hipster? Its desire to be 'alternative to the mainstream' – and here again, a definition by opposition! – and to strive for authenticity and uniqueness, two very broad and undefined terms. More substantially, who are the hipsters? Intuitively, we all know the answer, and it is based on a stereotypical mental depiction with few variants: people with extravagant beards and/or moustaches, wearing lumberjack shirts and beanie hats, travelling around on fixed-gear bicycles. But beyond stereotypical depictions, who or what is the hipster? Greif *et al.* (2010), then followed by many others, advanced the so-called 'hipster paradox': those who would correspond to the description of a hipster usually refuse the label of 'hipster', because that would massify them and undermine their claim of uniqueness and authenticity. Furthermore, in general culture 'hipster' has acquired a generally mocking and pejorative connotation indicating people that seek authenticity but are ultimately fake, whatever authentic or fake may mean in this context.[6] Following this logic, we should conclude that a 'hipster is he who refuses to be defined as a hipster, albeit resembling the stereotype of the hipster'. Hardly a satisfactory definition for the members of a subculture.

If you now have a headache, it is not your fault. At this point, the temptation to throw the baby out with the bathwater and dismiss the use of the hipster label entirely would appear very reasonable: the very existence of a subculture made of people who refuse to be considered part of that subculture is, at the very least, questionable, and it would constitute a marginal phenomenon, lacking any analytical relevance. However, what if it is not the hipster label that is useless and problematic, but rather its association with a subculture? My fieldwork, in fact, suggested so. The hipster label proved to be most useful to describe a common aesthetics and taste orientation embraced by an economy, its entrepreneurs and its customers, all centred on the experience of authenticity. Surely, some of the bartenders or food truck operators – and their customers – may recall more or less the stereotypical hipster, but they remained a scarce minority. These shops serve a more diverse client base and attract a wide variety of workers. As Ocejo argues in *Masters of Craft*, the main attraction of these jobs is their intrinsic contemporary *coolness* for (white, middle-class) individuals. Alessandro Gandini (2020) observes how cocktail bars and similar shops embedded in the hipster culture make the areas in which they gather the 'capitals of coolness of the Western world'. Notably, Gandini talks of 'hipster culture', explicitly opposing the conceptualisation of hipsterism as a subculture or counterculture. These shops, he argues, do not represent niche consumption trends, but a mainstream set of practices. Similar considerations can be made about hipsterism in the consumption field. The contradiction or 'paradox' between the characterisation of hipsterism as the will to be 'alternative to the mainstream' – intrinsic to the claims of authenticity and distinctiveness – and its mainstream contemporary status, is only apparent and emerges with more clarity when a genealogical approach is adopted.

Looking at Western society from the 1940s onwards, hipsters are only the latest of numerous *cultural milieux*[7] characterised by the refusal of 'mainstream culture', dominated by massification and alienation, and by the attempt to reach distinctiveness and obtain authentic life experiences. Indeed, Arsel and Thompson (2011) argue that the hipster label emerged between the end of the old century and the beginning of the new century as a 'marketplace mythologisation' and cultural branding of indie culture and economy. Before hipsters were cool (and the indie scene mature), David Brooks (2001) depicted the lifestyle of the 'Bobos in paradise', middle-class individuals who represented a synthesis between the new yuppie capitalistic ethos and the hippie, bohemian countercultural values. And this leads us to mention 'hippies', the American (and then Western) icons of the cultural revolution that started in the 1960s against all the most oppressive effects of capitalism in its Fordist phase on society and individuals. Hippies that, in turn, derived their name from the previous American subculture born in the 1940s whose members were named 'hipsters', in a *coup de théâtre* that brings us back – at least from a linguistical point of view – to the beginning of our brief excursus. As Tiziano Bonini (2014) explains in his detailed archaeology of the hipsters, the first hipsters were Afro-American Black people that developed a distinctive and eccentric style – expressed mainly through fashion and music – to affirm their Black identity. Shortly after, white people started to adopt the same label and appropriate that style to express their refusal to partake in the white Anglo-Saxon Protestant (WASP) American society of the 1940s. These 'white hipsters' constituted the matrix for the subsequent white countercultures of the 1950s and 1960s like bikers, beats and hippies. The words 'hippies' and 'hipsters' derive the common 'hip' prefix from an African-American Vernacular English word, which refers to being cool and authentic and at the same time distinctive and against the mainstream culture (Bonini, 2014). More appropriately, the prefix conveys the idea of being cool and authentic precisely *because of* going against the mainstream. 'Original' hipsters, beats, hippies, bobos, indies, etc., represent different generations in different decades that have wide-ranging peculiarities and differences – whose detailed exploration is beyond the scope of this book – but they still all share a common fundamental meaning, summarised by the original 'hip' prefix. However, the 'mainstream' of the 1950s and 1960s – *id est* the dominating sociocultural values expression of the capitalist economy of the time – was very different from the 'mainstream' of the most recent decades. To understand this shift, the focus must be set on the studies of capitalism as 'first and foremost a historical social system' (Wallerstein, 2011), connecting those works inspired by the Braudelian and Schumpeterian thought, in particular the regulation theory and Giovanni Arrighi's theorisation.[8]

The rise and fall of post-Fordism

The decade in which the global revolt of 1968 took place represented the apex of the capitalist Fordist mode of production, under the undisputed global hegemony of the United States. Fordism, based on the dual principle of mass production per mass consumption, guaranteed decades of growth and wealth first to the United States and then, especially after the Second World War, to European and Commonwealth countries, notably at the expense of the rest of the globe. It did so by transforming the competitive capitalism described by the classical economists and Marx in the nineteenth century into a 'monopoly capitalism', as per the title of the influential book by Baran and Sweezy (1966).[9] In it they observed that the core feature of monopoly capitalism was a systematic tendency of the surplus to rise, due to the price-setting capacity of companies in a condition of oligopoly, instead of a structural tendency of profits to fall (as argued by Marx with regard to competitive capitalism). Thus, the new endemic problem that capitalism faced was to effectively absorb and productively re-invest the economic surplus that it produced (Baran and Sweezy, 1966). As argued by Arrighi (1994/2010), during the 1950s and 1960s the United States and Europe experienced a phase of 'material expansion': they managed to absorb the surplus through commodity production, trade and consumption. Theorists from the regulation school (Aglietta, 1979; Jessop, 2001) highlighted how the good functioning of such a 'regime of accumulation' was only possible thanks to a 'mode of regulation' constituted by social institutions, norms, state policies and habits, that in the case of Fordism could be summarised under the label of 'Keynesianism' (named after the British economist John Maynard Keynes).

There is now a large consensus – even among very different traditions – that between the end of the 1960s and the beginning of the 1970s the Fordist regime of accumulation entered a crisis, triggering a systemic transition towards a new economic configuration. Indeed, in this particular temporal conjunction two phenomena occurred jointly: a crisis in the capacity of the Fordist system to absorb the surplus through commodity production; and, on the one hand, a connected growth in the magnitude of financial transactions, and, on the other hand, the beginning of a deep restructuration in the economic system of the Western economies that accompanied this transformation. In a systematic review of the financialisation of the economy in the second half of the twentieth century, Davis and Kim (2015) argue that this process is particularly evident in three levels: industry, firms and household. At the industry level, the US American financial sector's share of gross domestic profit (GDP) surpassed manufacture's share in the early 1990s; while at corporate level, the financialisation became visible in the new primacy of shareholder value in corporate governance. Greenwood and Scharfstein (2013) show that if in 1980 the total value of financial assets was five times the GDP of the United States, by 2007 this ratio had doubled: securities and credit intermediation were the main drivers for this spectacular growth.

The debate on the nature of the new economic configuration emerging from the crisis of Fordism has been variously defined as the post-industrial society (Bell, 1976), the knowledge economy (Drucker, 1969), flexible specialisation (Piore and Sabel, 1986), flexible accumulation regime (Harvey, 1989), disorganised capitalism (Lash and Urry, 1987), or more broadly post-Fordism (Amin, 2011), highlighting its different aspects and trajectories. In the present book, I will use 'post-Fordism' as an umbrella term. Apart from the (sometimes critical) differences, some points of general agreement can be traced in the debate: the seemingly inexorable growth of finance, the shift towards a more specialised and flexible production with a connected resurgence of small and medium-sized firms, the growth of the service sector and a diminished centrality of manufacturing, a rise in the wealth polarisation, and the growth in numbers and relevance of self-employed workers.

The renewed relevance of small and medium-sized firms led to the diffused hypothesis of a crisis of the corporation model and to a new triumph of Marshallian districts composed of networks of small firms. However, the reality proved to be quite different. In no economy did post-Fordism prompt the decline of the multinational corporation model, which constituted the core of the 'monopoly capitalism' under the Fordist accumulation regime. Instead, the model contributed to corporations restructuring towards a hybrid form (Harrison, 1998). This new organisational configuration was based on the outsourcing of all the non-core tasks and most of the material production chain to (networks of) smaller firms, while core immaterial assets and control over financial operations are maintained (Harrison, 1998). Despite the fact that the contemporary Silicon Valley ecosystem of start-ups has often been mentioned as an example of the strength of small firms and Marshallian districts in the contemporary economy, this is rather the result of a severe misconception. The fundamental goal of a start-up is to quickly accumulate as much venture capital as possible from investors to go from 'zero to one' (Thiel and Masters, 2014): from a small firm (that has zero value) to a monopolist company, able to saturate as quickly as possible a relevant and profitable market field. In other words, start-ups are successful only when they become monopolist (or oligopolist) companies in a specific industry.[10]

Furthermore, the currently dominant business infrastructural model of digital platforms is the translation in a digital economy context of the hybrid corporate model illustrated by Harrison as peculiar to post-Fordism: the platform outsources all the non-core tasks related to the production and provision of the actual products to small firms or freelancers, and maintains the core assets (i.e., in the digital economy), the ownership and management of the data (Srnicek, 2016). The digital economy – particularly after the 2008 global financial crisis – may have radically changed the landscape of the most valued companies in terms of market capitalisation, which are now the Big Five (Alphabet, Amazon, Apple, Meta, Microsoft) and digital platforms in general. But, if looked from a *longue durée* perspective – roughly the same time has passed between now and 1970 than between 1970 and the 1920 – this phenomenon can be analysed as the mature stage of a post-Fordist accumulation regime, with which it still shares its most fundamental features.

This transformation of the economy was possible only thanks to the rise of a connected new mode of regulation or governance in Western societies: neoliberalism (Harvey, 2007), which originated from the 'monetarist counterrevolution' that began at the beginning of the 1980s and epitomised by Thatcherism and Reaganomics (Arrighi, 2007, p. 172). The new post-Fordist regime of accumulation, supported by the new mode of regulation of neoliberalism, provided two decades of renewed miraculous growth for the Western economies in the 1980s and 1990s, still driven by financial growth. Arrighi defined this period as a new *belle époque*, whose beneficiaries were oblivious to their luck:

> The sudden and unprecedented prosperity that they had come to enjoy did not rest on a resolution of the crisis of accumulation that had preceded the beautiful times. On the contrary, the newly found prosperity rested on a shift of the crisis from one set of relations to

> another set of relations. It was only a question of time before the crisis would re-emerge in more troublesome forms.
>
> (Arrighi, 1994/2010, pp. 334–5)

Indeed, the core of Arrighi's theory is the notion that the financialisation of the economy experienced under post-Fordism – and the consequent temporary upswing – is not a novelty of our age, but a recurrent feature of each hegemonic cycle of capitalist accumulation when it approaches its demise. Before the US American hegemony, Britain was the epicentre of capitalistic accumulation (with its own regime) during the Edwardian era, and it experienced a similar pattern. The same can be said for the previous cycle of capitalist accumulation led by the Netherlands, which saw the role of finance grow tremendously during the end of their Golden Age in the eighteenth century (Arrighi, 1994/2010). Thus, for Arrighi, if we look beyond Western capitalism towards the world and we read again the transformations that occurred in the 1960s and 1970s, it will be possible to observe that the new hybrid model deriving from the interaction between large corporations and network of businesses led to rapid economic growth in East Asia more than anywhere else (Arrighi, 2007, p. 171). Thus, in his opinion, the most significant economic phenomenon of the second half of the twentieth century is not the development of post-Fordism in the United States and in Europe, but rather the economic resurgence of East Asia (Arrighi, 2007, p. 1).[11] Thanks to a reinterpretation of Smithian economic theory and the use of Kaoru Sugihara's thesis on the industrious revolution in China as a market-based, non-capitalistic economic development,[12] Arrighi conceptualises the new global hegemonic cycle of accumulation as a hybrid model that combined the traditional industrious, labour-intensive market economy of East Asia with the capitalist economy typical of Western societies (Arrighi, 2007, p. 171). More recently, Adam Arvidsson (2019) took up the legacy left by Arrighi by analysing how – in the new context of the digital economy – the industrious economy became a paradigmatic mode of production at a truly global level for both the digital and the manufacturing sectors. According to Arvidsson, this industrious economy is composed of labour-intensive and capital-poor small firms led by entrepreneurs willing to act as 'changemakers', and can therefore develop towards a new hybrid capitalist Chinese-led cycle of accumulation as well as towards a post-Capitalist market economy (or a combination of the two).

The dot.com crisis of 2001 and the global crisis of 2007–8, both of a financial nature, seem to have confirmed the prediction of the fragility of post-Fordist growth. Dario Gentili argues that neoliberalism's defining feature has become the 'art of government in the age of endless crisis' (Gentili and Pope, 2021). On a more general level, after the global financial crisis the signs that the post-Fordist cycle of accumulation is failing to guarantee levels of generalised wealth similar to the ones under Fordism are becoming particularly widespread. According to a report by the Pew Center (2020), in the United States the share of aggregate wealth owned by upper-class families has grown from 60 per cent in 1983 to 79 per cent in 2016; most of this growth has been at the expenses of middle-income families, whose aggregate wealth declined from 32 per cent to 14 per cent. The labour share of the economy is experiencing a continuous decline at global level from the 1980s onwards, as well (Guerriero, 2019). These trends have been famously illustrated and publicised by Piketty (2017) in his best-seller *Capital in the Twenty-First Century*, which has been highly praised even by neo-Keynesian and neo-classical 'mainstream economists' as Paul Krugman or Robert Solow, further demonstrating the diffused acceptance of its thesis.

Another good index of the substantial failure of the post-Fordist regime of accumulation is the generational wealth gap, which has become a critical feature of contemporary society. Today, millennials in the United States earn on average 20 per cent less than baby boomers did at their age (New America, 2019). Research based on Federal Reserve data that compared wealth owned by baby boomers and millennials in the United States at the same age found that baby boomers in 1989 owned 21 per cent of America's total net worth, while millennials in 2019 own only 3 per cent of it (Hoffower, 2019). Gandini (2020) captured the emotional consequences of this phenomenon by arguing that nostalgia towards a past 'good life' has become the *zeitgeist* of the present times. Older generations miss the 'good life' offered by the Fordist social contract between labour and capital, calling for a 'conservative nostalgia' that has fuelled the ongoing right-wing populist waves. By contrast, younger generations tend to express a form of 'progressive nostalgia', not towards Fordism but for a mythical pre-industrial era. This progressive nostalgia is expressed through the search for authenticity in every aspect of life and the ultimate goal to find some way to live a 'good life' in the interstices of the post-industrial society. This attitude, particularly characteristic of certain strata of middle-class young and middle-aged individuals, can also be considered the most mature manifestation of a tendency that had begun in that exceptional few years over the 1960s and 1970s, and that it is now possible to analyse properly.

From hip countercultures to the hipster economy

Overall, Fordism's demise in the 1960s and 1970s was not only a crisis in the system of production. Indeed, the Fordist system suffered at the same time a crisis of approval, which lead to widespread protests by significant components of the population, particularly the younger ones. This revolt against Fordism expressed itself mainly in two ways: first, as a critique of the working conditions under the paradigm of mass production; second, as a refusal to accept the cultural massification and oppression of society and the alienation of individuals, induced by the creation of a mass consumer society. In the first case, after the 'social contract' between capital and labour managed to maintain relatively low levels of conflict in the first decades after the Second World War, thanks to the rise in wages and the improvements in working conditions (Gordon, 2009), the second half of the 1960s saw a resurgence of social conflict (Crouch and Pizzorno, 1978). Notably, this conflict was led by the same new large mass of mass-workers that Fordism recruited in the two previous decades (Tronti and Broder, 2019). At the same time, in the Western world (and beyond) the cultural revolt against Fordism exploded, since its oppressive and degrading effects on individuals became criticised by a vast array of influential intellectuals too.[13] In the United States, the protests against the Vietnam war and in favour of civil rights brought to maturity the critiques advanced by the countercultures started in the 1940s. In Europe, the new mass of university students made possible by the labour-capital social contract of Fordism started both cultural and political revolts, that often intersected and allied with the workers' struggles. Boltanski and Chiapello (2007) argued that capitalism in its transition to post-Fordism reacted by fiercely rejecting the social critique to capitalism but incorporating, nonetheless, what they define as 'the artistic critique':

> on the one hand the disenchantment and inauthenticity, and on the other the oppression, which characterize the bourgeois world associated with the rise of capitalism. This critique foregrounds the loss of meaning and, in particular, the loss of the sense of what is beautiful and valuable, which derives from standardization and generalized commodification.
>
> (Boltanski and Chiapello, 2007, p. 38)

Furthermore, they note that this artistic critique was built on the interpretation of Marxian alienation not only as oppression on the working act but also as something that 'prevents human beings from living an "authentic" existence, a truly human existence, and renders them alien to themselves in a sense – that is to say, to their deepest humanity' (Boltanski and Chiapello, 2007, p. 52). In this view standardisation, disenchantment – in its Weberian meaning of rationalisation and bureaucratisation of society – and inauthenticity are strictly related. Boltanski and Chiapello affirm that what emerged from the middle of the 1970s was a *New Spirit of Capitalism*, as per the title of their book, an ideology that both legitimised and constrained post-Fordism, which replaced and updated the previous analogous spirit of capitalism that emerged in the 1930s in relationship with Fordism. The transition between one spirit of capitalism and the other is functional to capitalist restructuration, and it also ensures the consensus to the capitalist system in general when it becomes threatened by mounting dissatisfaction and critiques. The founding values characterising the new spirit of capitalism, to answer to the critiques of disenchantment, alienation and inauthenticity, were mainly 'autonomy, spontaneity, authenticity, self-fulfilment, creativity, life' (p. 504).

The definition of the spirit of capitalism as both legitimising and constraining features of a specific capitalistic accumulation regime is relevant to the scope of this book for a couple of reasons. First, thanks to its relative indefiniteness, the concept of the 'spirit of capitalism' captures some aspects of what post-Fordist theorists would call the mode of regulation and at the same time something else that I will define as the aesthetic regime of consumption. The indefiniteness allows for proposing a more dynamic model in which citizens, also in their role of consumers, can effectively constrain capitalism, obliging it to undergo restructurings. The mass of consumers is not portrayed as a mere passive victim of the processes of history. Consumption can therefore be inscribed more properly in the wider context of capitalism and attributed a proper relevance.[14] Second, it finally allows us to make sense of why it is in fact possible, as I did above, to propose hipsterism not as a subculture but as one paradigmatic aesthetics and ethos governing consumption – which accordingly contributes to shaping markets – in the post-Fordist society. I argue that there is a flaw, or at least a missing logical step, in the formulation that sees hipsterism as a subculture characterised by being alternative to the mainstream. Indeed, the 'mainstream' against which hipsterism fiercely stands is in truth the 'old mainstream', the set of values and features characterising what Boltanski and Chiapello (2007, p. 21) would define as the 'Second spirit of capitalism', the one legitimising and constraining Fordism, and the regulation school (in part) would define the Fordist mode of regulation. Surely Fordism has lost its hegemonic role, but it has not disappeared (and factories and blue-collar workers are still a relevant presence in society). Therefore, the old spirit of capitalism that fostered the artistic critique of the 1960s and 1970s has not disappeared either, and precisely because of this reason it can still be framed as 'mainstream'. But the predominance of this frame is, after all, fictional, as we already live in a society where authenticity has become one of the predominant paradigms that guide and organise consumption, as a consequence of the values propagated by neoliberalism and the new spirit of capitalism.

The better iconic example of this transformation is probably a juxtaposition of the two Woodstock events. In 1969, Woodstock became the icon of the counterculture that was shaking all Western societies (and beyond). The same three original organisers launched a Woodstock re-edition to be held in 1994, for the 25th anniversary, showcasing some of the original singers and the new leading generation of alternative musicians. This time, however, Haagen-Dazs, Apple and Pepsi were official sponsors. A lot of dedicated commercials and merchandising were created. MTV broadcasted the event live. This second time 'Revolution', notwithstanding Black civil rights activists' famous slogan, was televised – and as pay-per-view, too.

It is in this way that to be 'hip' (i.e., being cool, authentic and alternative) transitioned from being a defining feature of the identity of different (and subsequent) subcultures opposing the dominant (i.e., mainstream) system of values to gradually becoming a mainstream paradigm itself, embodied with varying degrees of intensity by large components of the contemporary societies, and in particular by the segments of the population representing the working backbone of the post-Fordist economy. Provocatively, the 'hipster paradox' solution could in fact not be to define a subgroup of people as hipsters against their will, but rather to recognise that – from the perspective of seeking authentic and distinctive consumption experiences – we all (or at least, most of us) are a little bit *hipster(ist)s*. To pick an example from the case studies informing this book, we display a hipsterist attitude when at the supermarket we opt for a product with a certification of origin and a biological label over a generic alternative; when we opt for a cocktail bar because it offers a distinctive list of exclusive signature cocktails and not the usual margaritas, or when at a restaurant we are positively impressed by a well-crafted menu with traditional dishes and highly sophisticated ingredients from a specific region (or even better, a city).

In the following chapters, this book will provide an overall analysis of the hipster economy in contemporary society. It will first provide a historically and sociologically grounded overall definition of authenticity, linked tightly to capitalism, alienation and industrialisation. It will then conceptualise the aesthetic regime of consumption as an analytic tool to read consumption phenomena together with the processes of capital accumulation and regulation, illustrating the hip aesthetic regime of consumption underpinning the hipster economy and the tight relationship between the hip and the kitsch aesthetics in contemporary society. Then, it will provide an analysis of the neo-craft industries as the purest expression of the hip aesthetic regime of consumption in late modern capitalism, the factors behind their resurgence and the related economic imaginary of consumption. The next chapter will introduce to the picture the neo-craft entrepreneurs as fundamental meso-level actors in the hipster economy and dealers of the authentic taste to customers. Finally, it will look at the hipster economy in the urban space, arguing how it constitutes an integral part of a new urban logic of the village, at the centre of many contrasting tensions in the development of contemporary cities.

1
A *longue durée* quest towards the meaning of authenticity

Authenticity is a word of ambiguous meaning and uncertain boundaries. Nonetheless, it has become a major paradigm, orienting taste and the aesthetic disposition of individuals in contemporary Western societies and beyond. 'The quest for authenticity', almost a leitmotif in academic treatises on the subject,[1] has become the holy grail of artistic, cultural and goods producers, the common denominator in all consumption experiences and (especially middle-class) consumers' lifestyles of the most disparate habits and tastes. Authenticity has radically transformed entire fields of consumption.

Heritage and tourism are probably the industries in which authenticity reached first a paradigmatic role, in a more open way. D. MacCannell (1999) already recognised it in 1976 with *The Tourist*, a seminal analysis of the dialectics of authenticity as the fundamental engine of tourism, rooted in a Marxian analysis of the (post)modern society. David Lowenthal, generally considered the forefather of heritage studies, put a huge amount of effort into his fierce critique of the dominant paradigm of authenticity in heritage conservation and consumption. Food and beverage consumption has been revolutionised by authenticity, particularly from the 1990s onwards (Johnston and Baumann, 2014). More so than in any other field of consumption, authenticity has become expressed in food through a more complex array of signifiers: typical, traditional, bio, organic, local, exotic, regional and genuine, to name only a few. Drinks are no exception, with craft beer representing one of the most successful commercial trends in recent decades (Brown, 2020), and the wine industries shifting increasingly towards 'organic', 'natural' or 'biodynamic' production processes. Today, the paradigm of authentic food has invaded supermarkets, too, with shelves filled with products crafted by marketing departments hoping to evoke an intimate connection with nature, the image of open fields and the countryside, the taste of genuine products from a past that everyone had feared gone. Private labels have adapted, too, with new dedicated product lines: albeit usually referred to as 'luxury' lines, the real trade-off that they offer for their higher price is an added aura of authenticity conferred through bio or local labels. In music, authenticity has grown in relevance to the point of becoming the reference point for producers and artists of all modern genres (Barker and Taylor, 2007). Every artist's goal is to attain fame, success and wealth without becoming 'fake' in the eyes of their fans, riding the wave of commercial success and 'pop' consecration, while plausibly 'remaining true to their original self'. The longer the ability to surf on this contradiction while demonstrating that 'success hasn't changed me', the longer the fame. In general, hip hop and urban music nominated themselves as the genre that incarnates authenticity more than any other: it does not top contemporary charts and guides the music taste of younger generations by chance. In their songs, rappers become the *aoidoi* of the tough reality of ghetto life and the anti-hero outcasts that carve their way out of poverty, overcoming mainstream laws and paths set by society; a remarkable co-existence of hip attitude, conspicuous consumption and conformity to the neoliberal ideal of the self-made man. In the complaints or 'beefs' among artists or crews, the main accusation towards one's adversary is to be a fake, one that raps about the ghettoes and criminal life without being a real *gangsta* or *from the hood*. Authenticity plays a major role not only in everyday music consumption, but also in live electronic music festival experiences – in *Dance Music Spaces*, Hidalgo (2022) analysed how, in such a context, DJs perform 'authenticity manoeuvrings' to counter the threatening stigma of commercialism, connect with audiences and rise in the artist hierarchies.

The idea of authenticity also orchestrates digital consumption in most major fields. To show one's authentic self and to consume that of others (whether influencers or friends) is the imperative of social media. The latest entry in the market, BeReal (who won the Apple app of the year 2022 award) included this mission in the title itself. Open Bumble, one of the major competitors in the dating app industry, to find an announcement encouraging you to 'Be your authentic self' by adding your values, allyships and interests, such as 'feminism', 'LGBTQI+ ally' and 'Black Lives Matter' as badges to your profile. Indie video games now represent a ubiquitous phenomenon in the video-game industry (Juul, 2019), exploiting the nostalgic wave using 8-bit pixel aesthetics and rediscovering old genres (e.g., adventure games). These games capture distinctiveness among users by exploring new, unique combinations between genres or by developing storylines with profound, melancholic, existential meanings. Authenticity also revolutionised another incredibly ubiquitous, and not-so-incredibly neglected contemporary field of digital consumption. The porn industry has seen the established oligopoly of video production companies bow to the new quasi-monopolist digital platform PornHub, with more recent platforms for sex workers or cam models – the most famous example being OnlyFans – adding themselves to this landscape. What PornHub and OnlyFans have in common – and the real reason for their dominion in the porn market – is that they intercept, foster and exploit incredibly well the new canon of amateur porn and modelling, thanks to the architectural infrastructure of their respective digital platforms. The consumption of amateur porn relies on its authenticity, as opposed to the fakery and standardisation of 'industrial porn'. Amateur models (claim to) represent a shift from the standardised aesthetic of the classic porn star towards a plethora of different, more authentic body types and physical appearances. Amateur porn videos (claim to) depict more authentic intimate intercourse, closer to real life scenarios.

With very little effort it might be possible to continue our anecdotical review of consumption fields in which authenticity has demonstrated all its mighty power for a very long number of words. However, it would be a useless task. The major goal of this book is to demonstrate that these transformations are not the phenomenon itself, but rather the symptoms, and that hipsterism as an aesthetic regime of consumption is paradigmatic because authenticity became a fundamental logic orienting taste and aesthetic discernment horizontally to single fields for the past 40 years. Such a task requires, first and foremost, to shed some light on the concept, until this point yet to be cleared even in this book; to explore what we mean by 'authenticity', presenting a detailed contextualisation and analysis of its meaning.

Modern authenticity, industrial alienation and culture

The intrinsic ambiguity of authenticity's meaning, its unbreakable resistance to any concise definition grasping its essence, has brought many to dismiss its utility entirely, with someone defining it as a hoax (Potter, 2011). Starting from the same premise, I shall argue the opposite. Authenticity cannot be reduced to a concise, satisfactory definition because it is a multi-faceted umbrella term that assembles a multiplicity of interconnected meanings at the centre of the everyday contemporary lived experiences of individuals. With a multiplicative effect, the more it spreads, the more people extend its use to other fields in which similar phenomena are happening. However, as often happens, the more the usage spreads and the more a univocal meaning is diluted, to the point of it being perceived as little more than a buzzword. Thus, despite the fact that it is still possible to analyse and define what authenticity means in a specific scenario,[2] a more general assessment about the meaning of authenticity in contemporary society becomes an impossible endeavour, if the analysis is limited to the past couple of decades when the effects of the new paradigm have become most evident. This issue also emerges clearly in a long list of works that have discussed authenticity with a sort of 'I know it when I see it' approach, employing a loose and unsatisfactory definition of 'staying true to oneself'.[3]

To pursue this different kind of 'quest for authenticity' in an attempt to grasp its general modern meaning, a *longue durée* perspective (Braudel, 1977) should be preferred. The structural transformations started in the 1960s are just the latest – and more critical – conjuncture in a much longer history of a bundle of feelings, stances and claims that we have come to call 'authenticity'. Two other conjunctures must be accounted for and brought into the picture. First, the (mainly Anglo-American) Romantic ethos against industrialisation – paired with modernisation and bureaucratisation, in its Weberian meaning – that began to emerge in the eighteenth century and peaked, with regard to the meanings associated with authenticity, with the Arts and Craft movement. Second, authenticity as the ideal reverse of Fordist alienation and the foundation for a freed, creative existence, as variously conceptualised in the twentieth century by a vast array of critical intellectuals. By analysing these two centuries, it becomes possible to group the disparate meanings associated with authenticity around some common themes. Overall, this chapter presents the assumption that authenticity acquired its modern meaning in opposition to industrial alienation, and the connected issues of commercialisation, homologation and standardisation. Thus, authenticity should be contextualised in the broader development of the concept of culture in opposition to industrialisation famously detailed by cultural critic Raymond Williams (1977) and coupled with the conceptualisation of craft in opposition to industrial production (Adamson, 2018).

In line with the *longue durée* approach, it appears necessary to start with a brief genealogical enquiry about the term 'authenticity' itself. The modern meaning of authenticity on which I will focus, stemmed from the only meaning that the word held for many centuries (and that is still widely diffused today), which is the quality of being the original versus a copy of an object. Lowenthal (1999) brilliantly highlighted this progressive expansion of the realm of influence of authenticity from 'exclusive concerns with buildings and artifacts' to broader considerations of 'ideas and beliefs', even if as a heritage scholar he used this assumption to criticise authenticity in his discipline, without deepening the analysis of this expansion process. Indeed, the fundamental shift linking the original meaning to the modern one happened when the ideas of 'the original' and 'the copy' translated from the material world of artefacts to the metaphorical world of the self. When Edward Young, a rather obscure English poet from the eighteenth century asked himself 'Born Originals, how comes it pass that we die Copies?' (Trilling, 1972, p. 93), so did all the generations thereafter. This is where the seed of a modern concept of authenticity was planted, in the metaphorical journey from authenticity as the original in opposition to the copies, to authenticity as the 'true self' in opposition to the alienated self. However, Lowenthal's remarks are a critical reminder that, in contemporary society, the two meanings have become so intertwined that they often become inextricable. A distinction between the two is useful at an analytical level, but it would be misleading to adopt clear-cut distinctions like the famous one by the American philosopher Denis Dutton between a nominal authenticity (as originality) and expressive authenticity (as consistency to the true self). This entanglement between two different meanings is probably best represented in the analysis of art, authenticity and aura by Walter Benjamin, where authenticity relates to an original artwork but constitutes an aesthetic quality that is expressed in relational terms. The authentic aura of a work of art, being related to a unique presence in time and space, exists only in relation to its related sensory experience. The loss of authenticity is the consequence of the alienation brought by the mechanical (industrial) accurate reproduction of aesthetic artefacts. The very nature of alienation intervenes, losing the predominant self-reflexive nature typical of Romanticism and acquiring a more explicit relationship to society and the masses: the Romantic *topos* of the man in front of the mirror is replaced by the image of the actor in front of the camera, from which the actor sees their image reflected but also confronts the masses hidden behind.

The Romantic ethos of authenticity

Starting the analysis of authenticity by exploring the Romantic movement has two fundamental benefits. First, even if in indirect ways, the Romantic conception of authenticity had a strong influence on current significant debates on the subject. For example, hundreds of marketing books for practitioners have been published exploiting authenticity's popularity, but given the paucity of authoritative, academic sources on the subject, books such the one by Lionel Trilling – discussing sincerity and authenticity in literary English novels from the eighteenth to the early twentieth century – tortuously became one of the major sources of reference for the contemporary debate on authenticity in marketing and branding (even if sometimes in a superficial way). Well before this book, another influential book discussing the Romantic ethos, *The Romantic Ethic and the Spirit of Modern Consumerism* by Colin Campbell (1987) influenced the marketing field, thanks mainly to its use by consumer research pioneer Russell Belk. Indeed, the Romantic ethos sustains a theoretical framework in which authenticity maintains an oppositional stance to the industrial mainstream without the need to adopt radical, often Marxist, anti-capitalist framings like the ones formulated by twentieth-century intellectuals, more problematic to adopt in certain debates and disciplines. This aspect, in turn, leads to the second benefit of including the Romantic concept of authenticity in the analysis. The idea of alienation immediately recalls the most famous, Marxian formulation regarding alienated labour, but an excessive focus on authenticity as framed by the Marxist traditional approach, and a 'New spirit of capitalism' perspective, runs the risk of essentialising its nature as a radical, counter-capitalist concept. The Romantic ethos of authenticity, instead, characterised by a more intimate and self-reflexive nature, creates a framework in which alienation can be presented as a broader and less politicised phenomenon, not limited to Marxists or radical readings.

In truth, it is possible to observe this multi-faceted nature of alienation in Marxian theory itself. Indeed, even if the first two types of alienation described by the 'young Marx' – the one from the products and from the production process – received much more attention, according to Marx industrial society also induced the alienation of man from other men and from human nature itself. For Marx, alienation did not just happen in the workplace, on the infamous assembly line in which the massified worker ends up being swallowed by the machinery. Alienation also derives from the fact that 'all the physical and intellectual senses have been replaced by the simple estrangement of all these senses, that is the sense of having', and that 'the less you are, the less you express your life, the more you have, the greater is your alienated life' (Marx and Engels, 1988). This kind of alienation, according to the young Marx, is fundamentally a consequence of the nature of money, which distorts the ability to be coherent with the true self, and potentially affects both the bourgeoisie and the proletariat, albeit in different ways. It is no coincidence, then, that the discovery of this broad conceptualisation of alienation – thanks to the publication of the *Economic and Philosophic Manuscripts of 1848* in 1932 – sparked the birth of so-called 'Marxist humanism', where most of the fiercer critics of Fordist alienation in the twentieth century belong. The discovery allowed some Marxist thinkers to draw a direct connection between Romanticism and Marxism too, most notably Marshall Berman and Michael Löwy, who observed that 'the first critics of modern bourgeoise society, of the capitalist civilization created by the Industrial Revolution were – more than half a century before Marx – the Romantic poets and writers' (Löwy, 1987, p. 891).

For the analysis of authenticity and alienation that emerged during Romanticism, the thoughts of three classic authors will be used as a source: Trilling (1972), Williams (1977) and Berman (1972). From their combined account, the Romantic movement and its stances appear tightly linked to the development of the modern concept of democracy and the process of industrialisation (i.e., with the birth of contemporary Western societies) (Williams, 1977, p. 34). Trilling (1972) is arguably the more influential author at the moment (at least inside the ivory tower of academic institutions); he provided a detailed analysis of the history of authenticity in the Romantic tradition, linking it to the historically antecedent concept of sincerity. Being a literary critic, Trilling hardly ventures outside the borders of literature, but his detailed treatise of Romantic sources shed light on many fundamental features still characterising authenticity today. First, authenticity has to do with the intimate human condition, with the inner self. Second, authenticity is a contentious concept, 'dealing aggressively with received and habitual opinion, aesthetic opinion in the first instance, social and political opinion in the next' (Trilling, 1972, p. 94). In short, authenticity demonstrates its full cogency when formulated in opposition to some nefarious phenomena. Furthermore, it does so by linking together the realm of aesthetic and artistic judgements with the world of social and political critique. A combined analysis of the last two points results in a clear dialectical dynamic, in which authenticity is a condition of the self, but that can only be reflexively conceived in relation to external forces that repress it, forcing humans into inauthentic lives. For the Romantic intellectuals of the eighteenth century, there is no doubt as to the identity of these special forces: the lust for possession and money on one side, and industry and its machinery on the other. The process that – in the eighteenth century as in the twenty-first century – requires the use of machinery and industries to perpetually increase the amount of circulating money is, of course, capitalism. The Romantic artistic ethos popularises another recurrent element of the contemporary critiques to capitalism and industrialisation: the commodification and commercialisation of every aspect of society – and particularly of literature and the arts – as a consequence of the new industrial civilisation, which reduces the artist (or more broadly, the intellectual) to a profession like all the others (Williams, 1977, pp. 38–9).

Inside the complex European movement that was Romanticism, the decisive influence for the development of the two opposite concepts of authenticity and alienation can be firmly identified in one of its most influential precursors: Jean-Jacques Rousseau. His ideas of authenticity and alienation are decisive to summarising the overall Romantic ethos. In his vision of authenticity, Rousseau juxtaposes to be *something* and to be *oneself* (Berman, 1972, pp. 168–71), linking together – as we would say using contemporary vocabulary – meaningfulness, self-expression and authenticity. He was the first author to present 'progress' and 'civilisation' as the fundamental forces that – through a dialectic mechanism – gave humans the ability to develop their 'most excellent faculties' as goodness, meaningfulness, aesthetic judgement, morality and knowledge, but at the same time prevented them from reaching the authentic expression (and knowledge) of themselves. For Rousseau the dualism between the alienated and the authentic self goes inextricably hand in hand with political and social oppression and therefore, as famously stated in the opening of *The Social Contract* (1762), 'Man was born free, and he is everywhere in chains'. Rousseau believes that modern society – epitomised by the life in the 'modern metropolis', which for him was Paris – allows everyone to unfold their individuality only to then repress it harshly, frustrating the expectations generated by these new horizons of progress. Pre-empting the theme of money as a source of alienation and of the commercialisation of art, Rousseau states that the modern individual's body, mind and soul:

> appeared as nothing but competitive assets, to be invested prudently for a maximum return; he was forced constantly to develop and perfect himself, yet unable, even for a moment, to call himself his own. The demand for authenticity, then, proved to be radically subversive of that peculiarly modern society out of which it grew.
> (Berman, 1972, pp. 313–14)

It must be kept in mind that Rousseau lived in the century in which the 'individual' as a subject burst onto the stage of history. This process was at the centre of the dialectical and contradictory combination of expression and repression. Rousseau illustrates the process in ways that would surprise the contemporary reader. A century before Georg Simmel described the blasé attitude of the citizens in front of the overstimulating modern metropolis, recognising the deepest problem of modern life as 'the resistance of the individual to being levelled, swallowed up in the social-technological mechanism' (Simmel, 1903/1961), and Émile Durkheim used *anomie* to describe the misalignment deriving from the passage from organic to mechanic solidarity due to industrialisation (Durkheim, 1897/1951), Rousseau lucidly observed the wake of these phenomena at work in the metropolis-in-the-making that was Paris. For him, the metropolis 'makes tastes at once more delicate and less uniform to the point where there are as many tastes as there are people'. Contrary to what we could expect from the author, that college textbooks monolithically depict as lost in the nostalgia for the pre-modern 'noble savage', Rousseau holds an ambivalent – if not positive – judgement towards this process: for him 'through disputes over taste, insight and understanding [*lumières*] are enlarged; this is how men really learn to think', leading him to recommend that 'If you have a spark of genius, go spend a year in Paris: you'll soon be *everything you can be*, or else *you'll never be anything at all*' (quoted in Berman, p. 168; emphasis by author). To reach full authenticity or to get caught and dragged along by the 'whirlpool of social life': these are the two extreme poles that the modern person must face, discovering in the city that they are an individual.

Despite the clarity of the depiction of the modern human condition by Rousseau, any attempt to draw from him a clear path to overcome alienation and reach authenticity would encounter significant obstacles. Rousseau expresses a much more variegated and less definitive array of considerations on this subject. However, it is possible to identify a fundamental motif: the achievement of authenticity can only be derived from a dialectical process that appeals to the pre-modern past, but at the same time is firmly rooted in the modern condition and looks towards the future. For Rousseau, the state of nature acts as one's compass, but he warns not confuse what is 'natural' in the savage state with what is 'natural' in the civil state (Rousseau, 1817, p. 406). In his own words:

> Although I want to form the man of nature, the object is not, for all that, to make him a savage and to relegate him to the depths of the woods. It suffices that, enclosed in a social whirlpool, he not let himself get carried away by either the opinions or the passions of men, that he see with his eyes, that he feel with his heart, that no authority govern him beyond that of his own reason. (p. 255)

Notably, the recent work titled *The Dawn of Everything* by David Graeber and David Wengrow (2021) adds an apparently odd but illuminating tile to the mosaic so far depicted. They argue that most traits attributed to the 'man of nature' – which form the basic features of authenticity for Rousseau and, reflexively, for the Romantic tradition – came from the critique formulated by Native American thinkers against the modern European society in the centuries after North America's colonisation. Sustained by a wide range of sources, Graeber and Wengrow demonstrate that Rousseau, the Enlightenment and Romanticism were decisively influenced by the critiques of individuals such as Kandiaronk – a Huron chief – about the lack of freedom and self-expression and the dependence on money of European societies, thanks to their coverage in a number of very successful *dialogues* compiled by missionaries and explorers. Thus, after remarking in the introduction that the Western idea of hipsterism was appropriated from Afro-American culture, Graeber and Wengrow's new insights could lead to the resounding conclusion that the contemporary Western ideal of authenticity derives from a cultural and economic critique of modern Europe by North America's indigenous peoples.

Rousseau was an important precursor in settling the fundamental meanings that Romanticists associated with authenticity and alienation. About a century later, the Arts and Crafts movement, born in the United Kingdom and later expanded throughout Europe, brought to full maturity a series of considerations and convictions that still deeply inform our contemporary understanding of authenticity as the opposite of alienation. John Ruskin and William Morris, the two most renowned Arts and Crafts theorists, never specifically mention authenticity. Still, the opposition between *mechanic* and *organic* society in Ruskin's and Morris's stated goal – that is, to promote a socialist consciousness to make workers 'understand themselves to be face to face with false society, themselves the only possible elements of true society' (quoted in Williams, 1977, p. 170) – substantially expresses the same tension. Ruskin further develops and reinforces the notion of the entanglement between the aesthetic and artistic critique, on the one hand, and the social critique, on the other. He believes that the two aspects are both applications of the same guiding principle: the achievement of 'wholeness of being' through the pursuit of 'typical beauty' (artistic standards) and 'vital beauty' (social standards) (Williams, 1977, pp. 146–50). Morris builds on these associations – and on his strong socialist conscience – to develop a theoretical framework that provides three pivotal contributions to our discussion. First, he puts the commercialisation of society in relation to the new industrial middle class, illustrating how the 'Gospel of Capital' operating at a macro level and dictating middle-class lifestyles ends up destroying the same artistic and cultural values for which the industrial middle class itself expresses great respect and admiration. The middle class, incapable of properly solving this complicity in commercialism, seeks refuge in either its acritical participation in the commercial logic to accumulate wealth, or in the formulation of a minority, a highly cultivated culture alternative to the one of the masses, which makes them aliens in their own society (Williams, 1977, pp. 163–5); moreover, the two strategies do not seem mutually exclusive. Second, the overcoming of alienation – that Morris explicitly depicts as overthrowing capitalism and establishing a socialist society – needs art to be applied to labour. In the author's words, art must 'destroy the curse of labour by making work the pleasurable satisfaction of our impulse towards energy, and giving to that energy hope of producing something worth the exercise' (quoted in Williams, 1977, p. 166), making art a quality of work. Such faith in art's corrective power with regard to alienation, represents the foundation of Morris's glorification of craft. However, as Williams notes, contemporary and subsequent readers of Morris misrepresented his thought as a *naïve* campaign to restore craft in place of industrial production in an attempt to portray him as a nostalgic thinker and sweep under the carpet his anti-capitalist agenda towards a future socialist society (quite similarly to what, according to Berman, happened to Rousseau, who was misrepresented as a pure nostalgic of the noble savage mythical era). These considerations bring us to the third contribution, that is the use of the past to inform visions of alternative futures. In Morris, the re-evaluation of the artistic quality of craft production and aesthetics – albeit partly nostalgic – is functional, not to the return to a pre-industrial modernity, but to the advent of a (socialist) post-industrial society, overcoming alienation by letting citizens freely arrange their work and to decide where machines can actually be employed as helpful, liberating devices (Williams, 1977, p. 167).

Williams (1977, p. 173) argues that Morris is the pivotal figure of the intellectual debate on culture and alienation in the nineteenth century, and his thought remained relevant into the middle of the twentieth century. This book – as the next chapters will make even clearer – demonstrates his right to the status of contemporary thinker in the wake of the twenty-first century, too: to employ the very fitting expression used by Chris Land (2018), Morris used craft to envision a 'movement back to the future' very similar to the contemporary neo-craft entrepreneurs. As such, Morris should be recognised as the true – known or unknown – patron saint of twenty-first century neo-craft industries.

Authenticity goes mainstream: the twentieth century

Through our analysis of the Romantic ethos of authenticity from Rousseau to Morris, we have discovered that most of the fundamental features characterising the contemporary understanding of authenticity were already present by the end of the nineteenth century. Authenticity emerged as a core concept at the intersection between the artistic and social critique to industrial society, the standard of a human life freed from alienation, and an antidote to the commercialisation and commodification of society. It became relevant by appealing to the past in order to depict potential visions of futures. Now, it is time to briefly turn our attention to intellectuals' understanding of authenticity in the twentieth century: this endeavour will add new, equally relevant layers of meaning, starting from a couple of premises. First – as in the previous section – I intend to adopt the viewpoint of intellectuals that had an influential public role during their lifetime, for their capacity to read and interpret the most relevant phenomena of their time and to influence a great number of people with their interpretations. Second, I will focus mostly on the period running up to the 1970s – that is, the beginning of the transition towards a post-Fordist economy and a hip aesthetic regime of consumption based on authenticity, as I will better argue in the next chapter.

With the development of Fordism, the alienating effects of industrial society became increasingly evident. Basically, Fordism had the same impact on industrial society as steroids have on a bodybuilder's body, exacerbating the negative externalities already present during the nineteenth century. Consequently, the ideal of an authentic life, and an authentic self as the antidote, gained popularity among a vast number of public intellectuals. Authenticity, whether expressed literally or with equivalent synonyms or periphrases, appears to be omnipresent in the thought of the critical thinkers of the twentieth century, who represented the main source of inspiration for the leading generation of the cultural and political revolts of the 1960s and 1970s. In their theories, authenticity represents the positive, conceptual opposite of alienation and repression.

In the monumental *Critique of Everyday Life*, Henri Lefebvre (1947/2014) states that 'man must be everyday, or he will not be at all'. To reach this status, one should reject inauthenticity and alienation by resorting to his inner self. Thus, authenticity is the opposite of these concepts, and can only emerge from the rejection of existential alienation: 'Alienation, now made conscious, and thus rejected as mere appearance and superseded, will give way to an authentic human reality, stripped of its facade, and liberated' (Lefebvre, 1947/2014, p. 170). Lefebvre himself notes that these ideas were also independently explored by the 'young' György Lukács, who developed the ideal of an authentic life in opposition to a 'trivial' (inauthentic) one. In *Escape from Freedom*, Erich Fromm (1941/2011) states that alienation commodifies human nature at multiple levels, the most devastating example being the commodification of one's own self and personality. This alienation can be overcome only through the achievement of 'freedom from' and 'freedom to'. The latter type of freedom is critical for one's realisation as a creative and active human being (p. 289) by developing creative and critical thinking and emotional, sensuous experiences (p. 313), which elsewhere he roots in the authenticity of the self. His fellow Freudian psychologist and member of the Frankfurt school Herbert Marcuse (1974/2012) criticises Fromm's approach in *Eros and Civilization*, and sets the tenets of a non-repressive society that would allow freedom and a new experience of being, based on the free play of human faculties and libidinal relations towards oneself and the environment. A similar ideal of an unalienated, authentic human nature plays a fundamental role in the thought of Noam Chomsky, who formalised it in the famous debates with Michel Foucault as:

> a concept of human nature that gives full scope to freedom and dignity and creativity and other fundamental human characteristics, and to relate that to some notion of social structure in which those properties could be realized and in which meaningful human life could take place.
> (Chomsky and Foucault, 1974/2006, p. 42)

Moreover, authenticity emerges as a fundamental guiding principle in works from outside Europe and pertaining to other disciplines. For example, in the *Pedagogy of the Oppressed* (1970) Paulo Freire analyses how the very essence of oppression finds its roots in the lack of existential authenticity: 'oppressed suffer from the duality which has established itself in their innermost being. They discover that without freedom they cannot exist authentically. Yet, although they desire authentic existence, they fear it [*because they internalised the oppressors' thoughts*]' (Freire, 1970, p. 48). According to Freire, individuals are able to develop authentically only when they become 'beings for themselves' through authentic praxis, education and organisation (p. 161).

Despite this impressive line-up of public intellectuals, every analysis on authenticity's meaning in the twentieth century would be incomplete without the inclusion of the existentialist thought of Jean-Paul Sartre, as complemented by Simone de Beauvoir, who was decisive for the popularisation of the concept. Sartre describes authenticity as the fundamental human virtue in *Being and Nothingness*. Still, he provides no definition of the term, apart from stating that it constitutes the opposite of bad faith (in French, *mauvaise foi*). As such, authenticity drives Sartre's existentialism through the exploration of its absence (Webber, 2013). Even in his subsequent works, Sartre merely provides examples of authentic ways of living, or of living in bad faith, without engaging in proper definitions. Since it comes directly from an existential philosophical perspective, his theorisation is the most abstract among those encountered up until now. Published in 1942, *Being and Nothingness* was written before the Second World War, which for Sartre, by his own admission, represented the apical moment of his politicisation (that marked his subsequent fame as a public intellectual). Given this premise, societal forces such as industrialisation and commodification remain largely absent from the picture. Sartre states that bad faith is akin to accepting an image of oneself that is inconsistent with one's own wishes. His exempla of the waiter and of the homosexual are explicative of this condition. Sartre uses the example of a waiter who paradoxically acts inauthentically because they behave too much like a waiter (i.e., according to the standards of what other people expect from a waiter, rather than acting on their own standards). Another example is the one of the individual who, after many sexual encounters with men, still resists the pressure from his friend to declare himself a homosexual. Consequently, it is possible to state by opposition that authenticity means to be consistent with one's own will and desires. Sartre connects deeply the idea of authenticity to the one of freedom, meaning to restrain or not restrain one's behaviour according to one's own decisions (Webber, 2013).

Simone de Beauvoir, in her work *Ethics of Ambiguity*, further develops an existential ideal of authenticity by arguing that to live authentically is to accept the ambiguity of existence but refusing to lose oneself in it, thereby reaching full consciousness of one's true condition. The conversion to an authentic life requires that one gives up the quest for the meaning of existence outside of themselves, and abandons any external absolute: 'Human existence makes values spring up in the world, and the undertakings in which it will be engaged can be judged according to these values' (de Beauvoir, 1948/1976, p. 15). Similar to Sartre's line of thought, but perhaps with a more developed theorisation, freedom plays a fundamental role in underpinning these authentic undertakings. If an individual intends to fulfil an authentic existence, freedom must be genuine: it must be used to dedicate one's own existence to others.

No genuine freedom and authentic conversion can happen for de Beauvoir if one's existence remains limited to itself (p. 67). Finally, in later writings, after his deep political conversion, Sartre himself – in a way that also seems to be influenced by de Beauvoir – also stressed the importance of structural constraints posed by industrial and capitalistic alienation: true, radical freedom and authenticity can happen only if alienation is overcome, a task that requires both a conversion in attitude and a revolutionary praxis to change the material conditions of oppression (Sartre, 1957/2009). By these means, he linked the existentialist system of thought to the Marxist humanist tradition of critical studies on alienation.

This brief overview focused on the intellectuals who exposed a critique of their present, linking it to a clear vision of a future based on ideals of authenticity. Most of these theorists pertained to Marxist – or, more broadly, leftist – traditions. Still, it should be acknowledged that when attention is turned only to the critical component, a much wider array of authors from different traditions enters the picture. These authors blame the conforming effects deriving from the centralisation and bureaucratisation of the economy under the rule of big corporations'. To name some of the most influential voices, Charles Wright Mills (1951) in *White Collar* condemns the social alienation deriving from the market mentality of Fordism and 'social institutions which by their bureaucratic planning and mathematical foresight usurp both freedom and rationality from the little individual men caught in them' (Mills, 1951, p. xvii), holding some nostalgic attitude towards the old age of small entrepreneurship and competitive capitalism. For him, the most representative character of the alienating 'advanced capitalism' (as he terms it) is the new salesman, who is neither detached nor creative as the old one. In *the Lonely Crowd*, David Riesman, Nathan Glazer and Reuel Denney (1950) described how modern organisation and bureaucracy hinder human nature, fulfilment and initiative by favouring an 'other-directed social type' that became dominant by superseding the inner-directed social type, limiting the possibility of individuals to fully know themselves (i.e., alienating them). The bestseller *The Organization Man* by William H. Whyte (1956), written mostly for a business and management audience, argued controversially against the collectivist ethics that he alleged was predominant in corporations, which favoured dull conformity and hindered individual creativity.

It is possible now to draw some conclusions from the array of authors that we have analysed so far. Overall, they share several elements with their colleagues of the previous century but introduce some relevant differences as well. Two main factors may help explain these differences.

First, we should consider the major influence of some theoretical traditions that came to prominence between the end of the nineteenth century and the beginning of the twentieth century: Marxism (and Marxist humanism in particular), Freudian psychoanalytic theory and existentialism. The second factor can be identified in the features of Fordism, which, compared to the developing industrial society of the nineteenth century, exacerbated the alienation of individuals on several fronts: pressure to conform, oppression of individuality and triviality of existence. The result of these factors is an ideal of authenticity based on the theme of freedom, interpreted both as freedom from conformity and oppression and as freedom of self-expression, the latter often expressed in terms of 'unleashing the creative human potential'. Authenticity remains a highly debated concept, used in the sociopolitical debate to unveil the harmful effects of industrial (Fordist) capitalism and to imagine radical alternative futures, but in the twentieth century it seems less related with aesthetic critiques of society – the kind of authenticity preferred by the Romantic tradition – and more with intimate psychoanalytic and existentialist questions.

The meaning of authenticity: a definition

The overview in this chapter spanned two centuries in the quest for an overarching, modern meaning of authenticity. The intention has been to adopt a historical, *longue durée* approach with the goal of explaining why authenticity has gained such widespread prominence in contemporary society. Many authors have remained out of the picture due to space constraints (and compassion for the reader). Still, it is worth trying to define a general model of interpretation for the concept of authenticity, a model that can overcome the narrowness of a specific sector (food, beer, tourism, music, etc.) or discipline (marketing, management, branding, etc.). Obviously, such an operation always involves a trade-off: formulating an overall interpretation, adding analytical depth to each of these specific fields and underpinning them requires a certain unavoidable grade of abstraction and genericity. The content of this final part of the chapter will also serve as a prelude for the next chapter, which will apply the model sketched here to analyse authenticity in the particular field of consumption, presenting it as the basis of an aesthetic regime of consumption characteristic of post-Fordist Western societies.

The first foundational element to recall is that authenticity can be properly understood in its modern meaning only if analysed in a dialectical relation to the alienation induced by the industrial society. Authenticity rose to fame and acquired meaning in reaction to and as the specular opposite of alienation, their growth in relevance happened in parallel, and authenticity developed its meaning by mirroring the transformations of Western industrial configurations. This is precisely the reason why authenticity has maintained such high levels of semantic ambiguity in its entire existence, from Rousseau to today, even in authors such as Sartre who put it at the centre of their ethics: it has become an umbrella term, whose meaning varies according to the negative externalities one associates with alienation. Even though such an origin, by contrast, may appear unsatisfactory, the *longue durée* analysis demonstrated its inevitability and coherence. Through the lens of Raymond Williams's cultural materialist approach, which states that culture should be analysed as a dynamic process shaped by formations, practices and institutions, the emergence of authenticity at the end of the eighteenth century should be contextualised as one aspect of the broader creation of culture in the same period. Culture's birth among intellectuals according to William (1977) is a direct consequence of the development of new systems of economic production (i.e., industrialism) and new types of personal and social relationships at the base of modern democracy. Thus, the idea of authenticity was developed as a reaction against a specific aspect of industrialisation and democracy, which was alienation. This is coherent with similar processes, too: when Glenn Adamson (2018) argues that the idea of craft, contrary to widespread assumptions, was actually invented in reaction to industrial production by the end of the nineteenth century, he describes precisely one of the effects of the growing popularity of the ideals of authenticity countering industrial alienation. This is the reason why, a century after the Arts and Crafts movement and contrary to all expectations, craft production has now returned to the spotlight of micro-entrepreneurs, consumers and academics.

Starting from this premise, the interpretation of authenticity that I advance is composed of three dimensions, each representing the ideal opposite of one face of alienation. The first, most fundamental dimension is related to the self and sees authenticity as the ability of autonomous self-determination of existence, as opposed to the conformity and massification of the self, operated by industrial capitalism. Here, conformity and massification hint at two similar but slightly different meanings: conformity is interpreted as the participation and acceptance of general and externally determined social norms, whereas massification is to be read as being indistinguishable from the mass of other people (i.e., the idea of being 'just another brick in the wall'). This is the dimension of authenticity related to Rousseau's notion of being oneself without being swallowed by the whirlpool of social life, Freire's ideal of 'being for oneself' and Sartre's and de Beauvoir's concept of refusing external absolutes in order to embrace one's own desires and will in autonomy and responsibility. This concept resembles more closely the original idea of being an 'original versus the copy' and the popular generic notion of 'being true to oneself'. From a historical perspective, this first dimension of authenticity is a product of the tension deriving from the interconnected birth of capitalism and industrialisation, which with one hand established the notion of the individual with rights and duties, and simultaneously, with the other hand, repressed it.

This chapter made very clear that the alienation of the self or of its authenticity is a condition that can derive only from the interactive relationship between individual agency and social structures, norms and institutions. In other words, authenticity can be conceived only as an experiential, practice-based quality. The fundamental dimension of authenticity of the self is conceivable only if related to two other dimensions of authenticity, referring directly to the two constitutive domains of alienation from the early Romanticists onwards: the pervasiveness of money and profit as the predominant – if not exclusive – founding principle of social life and the mechanic nature of everyday life induced by industrialisation.

Thus, the second dimension of authenticity calls for creative self-expression against the commercialisation and commodification of social life. This is the dimension to which Marx referred when he denounced the estrangement of physical and intellectual senses for the simple sense of having; the same aspect Morris discussed when explaining how the 'Gospel of capital' brings the middle class to destroy any artistic and cultural value, and which Marcuse and Chomsky hinted at when advancing a model of meaningfulness of practices rooted in creative thinking and free play. More generally, it is the kind of authenticity evoked by every plea to reach meaningfulness in the different realms of social life. It is the idea that any authentic expression of the self can originate only from overcoming the reduction of every practice to an economic transaction (commercialisation) and consequently of every entity of social life to a commodity (commodification). The third dimension, instead, describes authenticity as the distinctiveness of life experiences, against the standardisation and triviality of everyday life under the framework of industrial society. Even though the concepts of distinctiveness and standardisation are similar to autonomy and massification, the relevant aspect here is the experience of production and consumption, not the identity or the inner self. This fundamental opposition was illustrated by Morris in the contrast between artistic work and alienated work, or between the idea of craft and industrial production, and it also relates to the idea of authenticity described by Lefebvre as the exact opposite of trivial life. In this dimension, authenticity equates distinctiveness as the antidote to the standardisation of human experiences, which ultimately leads to the triviality of everyday life. These last two dimensions of alienation are clearly linked, but they do not necessarily overlap. In the Western societies of the past three centuries, the pervasiveness of money and of profit-oriented logic has developed alongside industrial production, becoming the defining features of capitalism as we know it. Still, it would remain possible to think of predominantly profit-oriented mindsets in a non-industrial society. In the end, both of the most authoritative theories on the origin of capitalism – Fernand Braudel's theory based on the development of Italian city-states in the fifteenth century, and Robert Brenner's on agrarian capitalism – place the birth and diffusion of the tendency towards profit for the sake of profit in pre-industrial societies. Equally plausible is to think of some kind of industrial production without capitalism: here, the examples are much easier to find, the most striking one probably being the (in)famous admiration held by Lenin towards Taylorism as the organising principle of industrial production.

To better summarise and clearly distinguish the different aspects of alienation from which each enlisted dimension of authenticity takes shape, it might be useful to recall the metaphor of the iconic hammers' march appearing at the end of Pink Floyd's video 'Another brick in the wall, part two'. In a harsh critique of the alienation caused by the education system, the well-known video shows an allegoric military march in which the participants are humans mutated into identical hammers, performing the goose step. The hammer-humans participating in the march are subject to massification, as they are all identical and indistinguishable from each other due to the external, structural pressure to conform. They are victims of commodification, as by submitting to the logic of capital (i.e., commercialisation) they are no longer humans capable of creative agency and have been reduced to hammers – mono-dimensional tools equipped to perform one single task (directed by those who hold the tool). They all follow the same standardised movement, at a rhythm imposed by others, with no possibility of distinctiveness from the mass, trapped in a trivial (and repetitive) life experience.

To conclude, it is necessary to recognise that in all these accounts – and metaphors – of authenticity the central element remains the idea of achieving freedom from all these alienating conditions. Adopting

Fromm's twofold conception of freedom as intrinsically both 'from' and 'to' something, the three dimensions of authenticity can also – and probably in a more effective manner – be summarised as follows: (1) *freedom to* autonomous self-determination, *from* conformity and the massification of the self; (2) *freedom to* creative self-expression, *from* the commercialisation and commodification of social life; and (3) *freedom to* distinctiveness in life experiences, *from* the standardisation and triviality of everyday life.

2
The hip aesthetic regime of consumption

In 1972 Marshall Berman published *The Politics of Authenticity*, depicting a compelling fresco of how authenticity had become a pervasive ideal in Western societies. In it, he argued 'our society is filled with people who are ardently yearning and consciously striving for authenticity' (Berman, 1972, p. 325). Who were they? Certainly philosophers and psychiatrists exploring ideas of self-realisation and ego-identity, as well as artists and writers shaping authenticity as a thriving cultural force. Still, authenticity was not just a concern among the narrow ranks of intellectuals and professionals or a generational fad for bored hip young individuals. Berman vividly expresses how the quest for authenticity had already become in his time a mass movement, composed of 'countless anonymous men and women all over who are fighting, desperately and against all odds, simply to preserve, to feel, to be themselves', by discovering 'a fact of life which our first seekers always knew: that whoever you are, or want to be, you may not be interested in politics, but politics is interested in you' (Berman, 1972).

More recently, Joachim C. Häberlen, Mark Keck-Szajbel and Kate Mahoney (2019) edited a homonymous book in which – focusing on European subcultures and radical countercultures – they notice how these groups attempted to live more authentically by 'joining consciousness-raising groups, listening to rock and punk music, or making bodies and sexuality a central aspect of politics' (p. 3). Apart from connecting the idea of authenticity to the rise of working-class and middle-class subcultures, they demonstrate that this uprising in the name of authenticity involved younger generations on both sides of the Iron Curtain. In line with the definition of authenticity adopted in this book, alienation as massification, commodification and standardisation characterised Western capitalist societies as well as Eastern communist ones.[1] These books demonstrate authenticity's multi-faceted and pervasive nature as it emerged between the 1960s and 1970s. Still, the *longue durée* path followed in the previous chapter made clear that this historical context was 'just' the moment in which discourses and sentiments about alienation and authenticity came to full maturity after a long gestation, like a subterranean river that after running and growing for miles underneath, finally springs to the surface in all its strength.

This chapter will narrow its focus on authenticity as the core value of a paradigm of consumption, orienting taste and consumption patterns in the past 50 years. To reach this goal, however, we must go beyond a plain descriptive analysis of 'the rise of authenticity' in consumption and develop a fine-tuned theoretical framework, where authenticity can be put in relation with taste and consumption patterns and contextualised in the wider processes of capitalistic transformations.

This chapter develops such a theoretical framework by conceptualising the 'aesthetic regime of consumption', with the aim of applying it to actual consumption processes and analysing the consequences for consumer studies. The goal of such a theoretical framework would be dual. First, it allows us to safely sail through the Scylla and Charybdis of 'productivist' and 'consumerist' reductionisms jeopardising such a journey by considering consumption as a mere appendix functional to the realm of production or portraying transformations in taste as something detached from the overall socio-economic transformations. Inspired by the regulationist approach – but overcoming its traditional neglection of consumption as per the productivist reductionism mentioned above – the aesthetic regime of consumption only makes sense if analysed in combination with what the regulationists would call the 'regime of accumulation' and the 'mode of regulation'.

The second goal of the developed framework is avoiding a frequent tendency in consumption studies; that is, presenting the consumer society as a totalitarian entity. Building a model capable of recognising structural power as well as the role of individuals' agency allows for a better understanding of the forces contributing to consumption transformations at the macro, meso and micro-level.

The aesthetic regime of consumption

In his *Vocabulary of Culture and Society*, Raymond Williams (1976/2015, p. 144) noticed how the widespread idea of mass production curiously 'does not really describe the process of production, which in fact, as originally on an assembly line, is multiple and serial. What it describes is a process of consumption, the mass market . . . a multi-headed multitude with purchasing power'. Despite this, historically, the field of consumption has seldom received comparable attention to its twin field, production. Consumption has often occupied a marginal space in studies concerning capitalism and economics, it has been framed as functional and made dependent on the organisation and orchestration of production. Furthermore, many of the sociological analyses focusing on Fordism as a consumer society (the two more immediate examples being the Frankfurt School and Jean Baudrillard) highlighted the relevance of consumption processes but treated consumers as passive entities, powerless in the face of the totalitarian shaping force of markets. However, if it is true that capitalist forces have a marked talent to co-opt any kind of emerging cultural trend – be it of trivial or critical nature – this demonstrates how such forces are pursuers as much as they are forerunners. Hence, what appears to be necessary is an analysis of consumer society that also takes into account its consuming subjects.

Luckily, more recently institutional and practice-focused approaches to the study of consumption have flourished. The concept of 'aesthetic regime of consumption' as a theoretical framework has been first developed by sociologist Jennifer Smith-Maguire, precisely by applying institutional and practice-based lenses to reinterpret the classic Bourdieusian theory of taste and aesthetic dispositions. Here, I build on her definition, albeit with some adaptations. Smith Maguire (2018a, p. 73) argues that the ultimate goal of her conceptualisation is to understand 'the practical implications of aesthetics and taste for the construction and operation of a particular market' by joining together 'the structuring frameworks for tastes and passions' and 'the tastes and passions of market agents'. The present book widens the scope of this goal and applies it to the study of capitalistic developments. The aesthetic regime of consumption is employed here as a theoretical framework aimed at understanding the practical implications of aesthetics and taste for the construction and operation of a particular capitalistic configuration, which is also composed of a particular regime of accumulation and mode of regulation. This relationship should be understood as mutual in its triangulation: the aesthetic regime of consumption influences the formation and operation of the regime of accumulation and conversely the regime of accumulation influences aesthetics and taste (at the same time, both influence and are influenced by the mode of regulation). Every analysis of one of these dimensions should take into account how tightly this mutual relationship is knitted.

The use of the term 'regime' explains the interdependency between the aesthetic regime of consumption, the regime of accumulation, and the mode of regulation. Still, what is meant by 'aesthetics' may appear to be quite vague. The idea of aesthetics is strongly related to the idea of taste: in one of its first uses, Sir William Hamilton defined aesthetics as the 'Philosophy of taste'. Ever since the term existed, to possess a sense of aesthetics has been construed to indicate the presence of a 'subjective sense-activity' distinguishing what is beautiful from what is not (Williams, 1976/2015, p. 2); for its part, in 1784 taste was already defined as 'the quick discerning faculty or power of the mind by which we accurately distinguish the good, bad or indifferent' (p. 247). The individual sense of aesthetics and taste, then, constitutes the fundamental ability underpinning every consumption pattern. Pierre Bourdieu (1984) incorporates the notion of aesthetic disposition to make sense of the core of his theory on taste: 'taste classifies, and it classifies the classifier'. Not only does taste allow us to operate judgements and distinctions between objects of consumption, but the taste embodied and displayed by individuals also leads to a distinction and classification of the individual by other individuals, as well. For Bourdieu, the aesthetic disposition is the acquired aptitude and skill – through domestic or formal education – to perceive and decipher the stylistic features of an object, focusing on its forms rather than on its function:[2] aesthetic disposition is what informs and steers the consumption of objects beyond their exchange and use value. The way in which the perception and deciphering process takes place also 'classifies the classifier': taste is a marker of social inequalities and contributes to their reinforcement and reproduction. Notably, Bourdieu adds that 'nothing is more distinctive than the capacity to confer aesthetic status to objects that are banal or even "common" . . . or the ability to apply the principles of a "pure" aesthetic to the most everyday choices' (p. 5): the aesthetic disposition can be exercised in every consumption activity, irrespective of its nature. Thus, the aesthetic evaluation expressed through taste – regardless of whether it is exercised towards high art or common objects – is not intrinsically determined by the object, nor by the 'human nature' of the viewer, but rather socially constructed. This implies that aesthetic disposition is strictly linked to structural forces and hegemonic notions of legitimate and illegitimate taste (or various shades thereof), to the point that 'any legitimate work . . . tacitly defines as the only legitimate mode of perception the one which brings into play a certain disposition and a certain competence' (p. 28).

Taking a step back to the conceptualisation of the aesthetic regime of consumption, the adjective 'aesthetic' highlights the fact that every regime of consumption is based on an aesthetic disposition that in turn it also propagates: aesthetic regimes of consumption are systems of reproduction of culturally hegemonic paradigms of consumption. It is possible to speak of an aesthetic regime of consumption only when an aesthetic disposition becomes paradigmatic of a particular capitalistic configuration, in co-ordination with a regime of accumulation and a mode of regulation. The hegemonic meaning and characterisation of an aesthetic regime[3] – and its persistence as paradigmatic of a capitalist configuration – depends on the outcome of a complex bundle of social relations deriving from the interplay between different, often conflictual entities, which cannot be predicted. This bundle is multi-layered, involving actors as small as individual consumers as much as giants like large corporations. Despite the obvious power of actors capable to operate at a macro level, individuals operating at the micro level can also influence the hegemonic aesthetic disposition at a collective level. Indeed, individuals embody the aesthetic regime of consumption because of structural constraints, but contribute to shaping its meaning as well, and this explains how the role of taste can be introduced more clearly in the picture. According to Smith Maguire (2018a), taste represents the aesthetic regime of consumption embodied by the individual: the act of tasting is the aesthetic regime in action. Thus, taste acts as the hook connecting the macro-level formation and transformation of aesthetic regimes to the micro-level of interactions between consumers and market actors, in their role as cultural and taste intermediaries. This is possible because, recalling the famous Bourdieusian notion of *habitus*, the aesthetic regime of consumption interacts with social actors in a way that makes them both internalise the aesthetic disposition shaped at the macro level and externalise their own practices arising from the socially embedded self (p. 75).

Bourdieu's theory of taste in *Distinction* explores the role of aesthetics and taste in orchestrating markets, shaping consumption patterns and reproducing social and cultural inequalities. However, the theory shows its weakness when the analytical focus shifts to the affective dimension of consumption: in other words, to the reasons why culturally hegemonic aesthetic regimes of consumption exert such powerful and wilful allure on consumers. Indeed, it depicts a social world and a human behaviour moved predominantly by self-interested calculation, aimed at the accumulation of power and (economic, social or cultural) capital whose function is establishing or defending class privileges. Mark Banks (2017) in *Creative Justice* proposes overcoming this impasse by building an original theory of practice juxtaposing Bourdieu's theory with

Alasdair MacIntyre's distinction between the internal and external goods of practices. While the external goods of a practice (money, reputation, social status, etc.) are instrumental to competitive, self-interested goals, MacIntyre argues that internal goods are just as relevant in determining individuals' agency (and even more pivotal for understanding personal realisation): internal goods refer to intrinsic, pleasurable rewards that can only derive from the immersion in the specific practice and for the sake of the practice itself (this distinction will also be relevant later on in the discussion about neo-craft industries).

The consideration of internal goods and the intrinsic affective rewards deriving from consumption practices appears fundamental in order to formulate a complete model of aesthetic regimes of consumption. In an attempt to reach this goal, without undermining the overall theoretical framework or further complicating it, the late Bourdieu himself may lend us a helping hand in the *Pascalian Meditations* (1997). Here, Bourdieu fully develops his theory of symbolic capital, defining it as the function that any other type of capital (economic, cultural, social) assumes when publicly recognised by others as a legitimate and distinctive sign of importance and reputation. The symbolic capital maintains for Bourdieu a clear instrumental and extrinsic value: humans accumulate it under the form of reputation – through the accumulation of the other forms of capital – to compete with and surpass other people's social prestige in the social arena. Still, the translation of other types of capital into symbolic capital provides both extrinsic *and* intrinsic rewards. By resorting to Pascal's thought, Bourdieu acknowledges that 'there is happiness in activity which exceeds the visible profits – wage, prize or rewards – and which consists in the fact of emerging from indifference, being occupied, projected toward goals, and feeling oneself objectively, and therefore subjectively, endowed with a social mission' (p. 240).[4] Symbolic capital is what provides individuals with a 'reason for being' and makes them important in their own eyes: this type of capital has the power of giving meaning to life, rescuing it from insignificance. Given that it touches on the most intimate dimensions of life, Bourdieu attributes the utmost importance to symbolic capital: 'one of the most unequal of all distributions, and probably, in any case, the most cruel, is the distribution of symbolic capital, that is, of social importance and of reasons for living' (p. 240). Even if in *Pascalian Meditations* Bourdieu pays only fleeting attention to matters of taste and consumption, integrating his late theorisation of symbolic capital into his theory of distinction is a quite straightforward operation. Individuals mobilise and incorporate aesthetic dispositions in the consumption experiences also because they add affective and symbolic meaning to the consumption process; ultimately, this too becomes a pleasurable and rewarding experience in itself.

In summary, aesthetic regimes of consumption can be defined as having three fundamental features: they are embodied by every individual, but exist independently from anyone; they form and reproduce culturally hegemonic aesthetic dispositions and taste, setting the boundaries between legitimate and illegitimate systems of appreciation and evaluation; and they have the power of orchestrating consumption horizontally through industries, because they develop in connection with broader capitalistic configurations. They are internalised and employed by consumers, in various forms and combinations, due to the combined structural influence of macro forces and their capacity to enable the accumulation of symbolic capital, which translates into the achievement of reputation and distinction from other social groups or classes on one side, and affective, pleasurable rewards and meaningfulness on the other.

Still, it is important to stress that the aesthetic regime of consumption remains a heuristic concept created with the goal of deepening the analysis of taste, consumption processes and capitalistic transformations in society. In doing so, it is best suited for capturing essential, overall features, rather than accounting for peculiarities. It is not a tool for societies' essentialisation (and trivialisation). In other works, Smith Maguire applies the metaphor of gravity (2019): as with gravity, the power of the aesthetic regime of consumption may be secondary when looking at the level of consuming micro-interactions. Such power affects consumption patterns, but does not steer them, with other factors holding a more decisive influence. However, if we zoom out to look at the broader picture and shift to the macro level of analysis, the aesthetic regime of consumption's gravitational pull 'may be the most significant force behind the fact that individual decisions of thousands, or tens of thousands, or hundreds of thousands of geographically disparate consumers wielding an infinite diversity of interests nevertheless accrete into an identifiable pattern' (p. 207). These observations do not reject the complexity and significance of a wide array of glocal socio-economic factors in shaping individual consumption habits: they shed light on the underlying forces causing the formation and establishment of overarching tendencies in taste that can be traced across different industries and cultural contexts. The three vignettes in the introduction about cocktail bars in Milan, New York and Tokyo are powerful examples of this concept.

The hip aesthetic regime of consumption

In 1963, Pepsi launched 'Pepsi generation', a bold branding campaign aimed at gaining terrain against Coca-Cola: the focus of the strategy was to frame Pepsi consumption as a feature of a young, rebellious and cool *lifestyle*. 'Come alive!' incited the song in the commercial before the voice-over clarified: 'Who is the Pepsi generation? Just everyone with a young view of things, active livelier people.' Pepsi was among the first companies to understand the inherent commercial potential of the new hip countercultures and to exploit them, and they would re-launch new versions of the campaign over the following decades. In 2001, a re-staging of all the commercials celebrated the 'Pepsi generations': riding the first signs of a nostalgia wave, too, Pepsi claimed to be the drink of every generation of cool, hip rebels. In 1971, Coca-Cola fought back by launching the 'Buy the world a Coke' campaign, destined to become one of the most iconic examples in advertisement industry – and chosen as the end footage of the television series *Mad Men* to represent the beginning of a new advertising era. The commercial's goal was to align the Coca-Cola brand with the aesthetics of the (by then already mature) hippie love culture. In the 'burger wars' between McDonald's and Burger King, the other great food 'war' animating the United States in the same period, Burger King began in 1974 by building its brand identity around the tagline 'Have it your way', and emphasising the personalisation of Burger King products as opposed to the standardisation of McDonald. The same tagline accompanied the new launch of Burger King in 2002, with variants in 2014 ('be your way') and 2022 ('You rule') insisting on the same concept.

A decade later and in a very different industry, Apple officially launched its first MacIntosh through the celebrated '1984' commercial, in which a totalitarian society populated by dull, all-identical grey-scale humans guided by Big Brother's voice gets (literally) shattered by a colourful, young and rebellious athletic woman holding a giant hammer, chased by a horde of riot police. The same message is conveyed through the 1997 tagline 'Think different', on which Apple built its relaunch and tremendous brand value. Again, another example from another industry: in 1987, Nike built the foundations for its leadership in the shoe and apparel industry by proposing the tagline 'Just do it' and launching an incredibly successful commercial featuring the iconic 'revolution' song by the Beatles, a symbol – albeit controversial – of countercultural revolt: the surviving Beatles sued the company (Bradshaw & Scott, 2018).

All these taglines and campaigns defined the identity of some of the most valuable brands in Western economy from the 1970s until today. They show the predominance of the general values of self-determination, self-expression and distinctiveness; precisely the tenets of authenticity illustrated in the last chapter, not only across many different decades but across very different industries, as well: from food and beverages, to computers, to apparel. These values are expressed through recurrent strategies, such as the integration of hip aesthetic – as illustrated in the introduction – based on being cool thanks to the distinction from – and against – mainstream societal norms, or the determination and expression of the individual self through the adoption of personalised consumption experiences and lifestyles.

The transition from Fordism to a flexible regime of accumulation offered a way out from the ongoing surplus accumulation issue, represented a reaction to the widespread protests of those years and captured the emerging changes in people's taste, at the same time also accelerating these same phenomena. By promoting ideals of freedom, individuality, creativity and enterprise (in both its meanings), the neoliberal mode of regulation reinforced, and was reinforced by, taste transformations. These transformations triggered a paradigmatic shift in marketing that neither anticipated nor followed this dynamic, but instead developed in parallel to these processes, as clearly demonstrated by the Pepsi Generation commercial from 1963. In the seminal article where the concept of 'marketing segmentation' was coined, Wendell Smith (1956) observed that marketing's predominant goal of favouring the convergence of people's taste towards a standardised aesthetic was the 'marketing counterpart to standardisation and mass production in manufacturing'. However, he added, 'In some cases, the marketer may determine that is better to accept *divergent* demand as a market characteristic and adjust product lines and marketing strategy accordingly'. Adam Arvidsson (2006) points out how, during the same period, the application of psychoanalysis to marketing led to the growth of market motivation, shifting the focus onto the self-expression of customers: leading figures such as Ernest Dichter recognised in *Discovering the Inner Joneses* that the US middle class was turning to an aesthetic 'to please the inner man' (Arvidsson, 2006).

The title of Dichter's article was a twist on a common English idiom, to 'keep up with the Joneses', which referred to the widespread goal during the economic boom to improve one's own living standards and prestige at the same rate as one's peers (the Joneses being the ideal-typical neighbours). The same psychoanalytic theories that fostered the ideas of authenticity and the critique of Fordist alienation were used as a foundation for this new marketing paradigm. But obviously, focusing the attention on the 'Inner Jones' did not mean putting an end to the will of accumulating symbolic capital in the social arena; it simply led to a transformation of its nature. Resorting to the same semantic twist, Don Slater (1997) argued that the ever-expanding influence of marketing under the new heralds of market segmentation and motivation research (and, more generally, of consumer behaviour) made post-Fordist consumer culture all about 'keeping different from the Joneses'. 'Discover the inner Jones' and 'keep different from the Joneses' became the two main tenets of the new symbolic capital to which consumers aspired. The two aspects are connected: the focus on the inner self – with a freely determined individuality – can only be expressed in the social arena through one's distinctiveness from others. The contradiction immediately stands out: in this context, authenticity soon acquires a normative dimension, and it inevitably leads to new – albeit different – types of conformity. To express this difference, Luc Boltanski and Eve Chiapello (2007) argued that post-Fordism substituted standardisation with the *codification* of legitimate aesthetics of consumption. Similarly, Sharon Zukin in *Naked Cities* highlighted how the imperative of an authentic urban life, chasing the goal of valorising the distinctiveness of urban places, perversely turned into a death sentence for any peculiarities and rendered urban places indistinguishable (see also Chapter 5 of this volume).

The finest analysis of the appearance of the hip aesthetic regime between the 1960s and 1970s is arguably *The Conquest of Cool* by Thomas Frank (1997), which represents a formidable companion to *the Second Spirit of Capitalism* because it recounts how the two worlds of counterculture and corporate environment were mutually intertwined. The counterculture was inspired by celebrities and rockstars, coming from the commercial media and cultural industry of the time; on the corporate side, marketing transformations were often led by new marketers who sincerely thought of countercultures as allies against a common enemy, identified in pervasive conformity. Only by recognising this iterative process is it possible to understand 'the story of hip's mutation from native language of the alienated to that of advertising' (p. 8). The rise of a hip aesthetic regime of consumption was a wide sociocultural change, of which the explosion of countercultures and marketing transformations were mere expressions. Were the Beatles more a symbol of counterculture, or rather an example of capitalist creation and co-optation of new consumer culture? They were both, and this ambiguity is intrinsic to the process, as Thomas Frank reminds us.

Surely, at the centre of the new hip aesthetic regime of consumption was the concept of lifestyle, which well summarised the new aspiration towards self-determination, self-expression and distinctiveness from others (Featherstone, 2007). Every exhibited element of the self, from body features such as fitness, hairstyles and tattoos, to practises like eating, drinking and music listening, became functional to the expression of the individual's highly personalised taste and identity, more than ever before. Subcultures and countercultures quickly became the most visible manifestation of these trends oriented towards the affirmation of one's own individuality against the massified mainstream culture. Matters of aesthetics, social status, preferences and beliefs all converged in forging a unique identity, which was also a cultural and political statement to the outer world. Still, subcultures showed the same ambiguity mentioned before: born to distinguish – often vehemently – its members from the massified, commercialised culture, they almost inevitably ended up going through the same fate of commercialisation – at least as a lifestyle, if not as a culture.

Mainstream, capitalist institutions almost always treated subcultures with the same twofold reaction: on one side they depicted them as new 'folk devils' (Marchi, 2014) to instigate continuous waves of moral panic against them; on the other, they tweaked their aesthetics and washed away any trace of anti-capitalist remnants for market purposes. More precisely, capitalist institutions were able to exploit subcultures for their own marketing only thanks to the first step: the demonisation of the subculture was essential to maintain an aura of hipness and rebellion, the very basis of its commercialisation under a hip aesthetic regime. No subculture escaped the commercialisation of its aesthetics, something which is probably most visible when looking at musical genres: sooner or later, the music industry managed to add the 'pop-' prefix to any genre. Let us take punk, one of the most radical subcultures emerging in the 1970s. It is relatively easy to trace a path that starts in the 1970s, with musical groups such as Clash and Crass, passes through the 1990s when groups like Green Day, Offsprings, Blink-182 and Sum 41 launched a new pop-punk mania, and ends in the first years of the new millennium with (pop-)pop-punk celebrities such as Avril Lavigne. However, the same ambiguity can be traced back to the very origins of the movement, when the Sex Pistols' brief stage life was characterised by the controversial relationship between its members' authentic punk attitude and the clever commercial strategies arranged by their manager Malcolm McLaren. As Sarah Thornton observed in *Club Cultures* (1995), mainstream media and cultural industries have been part and parcel of subcultures right from their beginning.

Even when analysing Western consumer cultures and marketing strategy with a bird's eye view, flying over the obvious plethora of contextual declinations, contaminations and developments, a hip aesthetic regime of consumption has clearly remained paradigmatic of the post-Fordist capitalist configuration over the decades, reaching the phase of full maturity: the array of cases provided in the introduction Chapter 1 supports this interpretation. Not only is a hip aesthetic at the base of the centrality acquired by 'craft' in contemporary economy and marketing, both as a quality to be possessed and as a process to enact; moreover, a hip aesthetic inspires a great number of (young, middle-class) individuals to become small entrepreneurs with ethical goals; it dominates economically and visually the urban retailing economy of contemporary cities – particularly in their 'coolest' neighbourhoods – with significant consequences and challenges. An authentic, hip subculture has also been instrumental in the development of Silicon Valley's cyberculture and the 'Californian ideology', on which contemporary digital society is based (Turner, 2008).

Still, during these decades a fundamental shift took place in the way the hip aesthetic regime of consumption works: the rising importance of matters of ethics and 'politics' for taste. On one side, this may seem like a natural consequence of an aesthetic regime based on authenticity that, as extensively argued, constituted from its origin a controversial concept combining political and aesthetic critiques of the present. Furthermore, once the consumption experience became a constitutive element of individual self-determination, expression and distinction from others, all matters pertaining to ethics, politics and morality entered into the taste sphere more explicitly. This phenomenon led to the so-called 'political consumerism', by which citizens consider taste choices as a form of activism. But in line with the same trend observed for every hip subculture, the capitalist aesthetic regime assimilated these instances (albeit with some delay). The process did not happen overnight – for at least a couple of decades the neoliberalist regulation mode pushed forward a concept of 'individual' and 'self-realisation' that marginalised these issues. Theses about the end of history and the obsolescence of ideologies became widely popular. In Italy, a clever expression was coined to describe this phenomenon: 'the ebb to the private sphere'. Finally, a combination of historical processes countered the trend, and that again demonstrates the usefulness of reading capitalist configurations in their overall development. In the 1990s, a new wave of global movements – which ultimately gave origin to the World Social Forum – started to protest against neoliberalism. From the *Selva Lacandona* in Chiapas, to *Puerto Alegre* in

Brazil, to the whole world, the movement denounced that the globalised 'flexible production' still translated into vast deals of exploitation and alienation, particularly for the poorer ends of the new global production chains; that no matter how much food consumption may have become tailored to personal taste, food multinationals were still destroying biodiversity and menacing local communities; that the bond between the self, identity and consumption only further increased the commercialisation and commodification of human life.

The strength of this global movement of protest faded after the turn of the millennium, but history quickly proved the major significance of their arguments. The dot.com crash of 2002 and the 2008 global crisis,[5] the gravity of looming ecological collapse, the unveiling of corporate violence particularly in the Global South, and the persistence of widespread racial and gender inequality, all forced capitalism to gradually account for these topics with a new parallel process of incorporation of some instances and harsh repression of others. At the same time, the business approaches that – again, not by coincidence – originated between the 1960s and 1970s (i.e., corporate social responsibility and stakeholder theory) came to full maturity after a long development, providing the perfect foundations to perform this shift: the approaches stipulate that companies must develop ethical strategies and contribute to tackling social issues, considering the interests and the wellbeing of all the stakeholders affected by the externalities of business operations. The outcome is what commentators and academics alike are starting to frame as 'woke capitalism' (Rhodes, 2021), which seems to be emerging as a potential new mode of regulation, in response to the endless crisis of neoliberal capitalism. The analysis of woke capitalism's significance and developments is a topic for another book. What matters here is how the hip aesthetic regime of consumption based on authenticity aligns with the new tenets of woke capitalism, despite a number of challenges and contradictions that are particularly evident when comparing big firms incorporating a corporate woke approach with the diffused industrious economy of 'changemakers' animating small local firms (Arvidsson, 2019; Bandinelli, 2019); these aspects will be analysed further in the next chapters.

The authentic and the kitsch

An aesthetic regime of consumption varies over time and space, manifesting itself in several variations. It evolves together with wider socio-economical temporal and geographical transformations. When the capitalistic configuration to which it is connected is shaken, it can enter a crisis too, losing its paradigmatic status in favour of other regime(s). Still, it will arguably remain a relevant presence in society: different aesthetic regimes related to different capitalistic configurations do co-exist in society, shaping and being shaped by societal actors with varying intensities and combinations. As seen so far, the hip aesthetic regime of consumption is rooted in the notion of it being 'alternative to the mainstream', and this foundation is consistent with the reliance on authenticity that has historically acquired meaning by contrast. But what is actually considered 'mainstream'? To find an answer to this question, it is necessary the gaze once again towards the historical horizons of the analysis and turn our attention to the Fordist capitalist configuration, thereby acknowledging that Fordism not only had a regime of accumulation and a mode of regulation, but that it also had a distinctive aesthetic regime of consumption, too. This Fordist paradigm of consumption should not be looked for in highbrow culture, but rather on the progressive aestheticisation of lowbrow taste: in one word, in the 'pop' or the 'kitsch'.

More than the famous American Pop art movement of the 1960s, it is the early British pop art movement Independent Group that proves useful. Artists and critics such as Eduardo Paolozzi, John McHale and Lawrence Alloway turned their attention to pop standardised products of consumption – often thanks to their shared working-class roots – as cultural objects with a specific 'pop' aesthetic aura, which turned into tools both for the massification of society and for the enjoyment and empowerment of consumers' living standards. Social theorists working at the intersection between culture, economy and aesthetics often preferred to employ the label 'kitsch', which was born and popularised to describe every possible degeneration suffered by art and aesthetic forms of consumption during the twentieth century. Some iconic examples of kitsch aesthetics are mass-produced clothes made of poor materials and blunt design; flashy accessories; home furniture or decorations with trivial style; touristic cheap souvenirs; low-quality music based on excessive sentimentalism; cheap art designed to easily attract popular taste. On a more formal, generalised level, the term kitsch evokes a varied but coherent set of properties related to an ordinary, massified, trivial and commodified aesthetic: everything that is *inauthentic* (Belpoliti, 2020).[6]

Sociologist Norbert Elias (1935) was among the first and most lucid thinkers to elaborate on the relationship between kitsch as aesthetics and capitalism, by writing that 'the term kitsch is one of the very few capable of signalling a common trait to all the aesthetic products of capitalism'. The same tension recognised by pop art critics is acknowledged by

Elias, too: he describes how 'the kitsch represents the escape dream of a workers' society . . . The individual art specialist is powerless in front of the compulsiveness with which professional life pushes the recreational activities of the industrial man in very specific directions'.

Interpreting it as an aesthetic regime, the pop or kitsch aesthetics makes sense only if connected to the development of Fordism and the industrialisation of culture: it is both functional to a Fordist regime of accumulation and a Keynesian mode of regulation, and necessary for their functioning. The mass, standardised production of objects must develop together with a standardised and simple aesthetic, easily reproducible through industrial means. The Keynesian welfare state, aimed at achieving full employment and rising the mass of workers' purchasing power in order to guarantee a demand high enough that it can absorb mass production, must develop in parallel with an aesthetic that can be transferred to cheap products and appreciated by the cultural schemes of the working class. If the hip aesthetic regime of consumption's most representative consumer object is the craft(ed) product, the pop or kitsch iconic consumer object is the industrial(ised) product. Pop became an aesthetic regime adopted by the working class leading the economic boom under Fordism, but existing independently from it (and from Fordism itself), strong enough to provoke a gravitational force of consumption in the most disparate industries.

Its diffusion depended on economic and cultural institutions that, as Stuart Ewen described in *Captains of Consciousness* (2021), developed advertisement and marketing from the 1920s onwards as 'aggressive devices of corporate survival' aimed at manufacturing consumers in the same way in which they manufactured products. A pop, kitsch aesthetic was perfect for this process of marketing engineering. In his famous discussion of masscult and midcult, Dwight Macdonald (2011) defined these forces as 'the Lords of the kitsch', underlining how, from an aesthetical perspective, kitsch is a vulgarised by-product of highbrow culture as well as an elevation of popular culture. Kitsch is the aesthetics of a proud working class that seeks to demonstrate to the rest of society its improvements in social status through mass consumption. As the philosopher Thomas Kulka (1996) observed, 'If works of art were judged democratically – that is, according to how many people like them – kitsch would easily defeat all its competitors'. To consider kitsch as a source of distinction may well sound like a paradox, as the term itself originated in highbrow society to create a distance from the 'vulgar' masses. The thought of the industrial object possessing a powerful allure today may seem absurd. Has not the idea of authenticity – as argued in the previous chapter – come precisely from a protest movement against everything that kitsch represents? Still, pop aesthetics holds symbolic capital just like hip aesthetics, although in a different code.

The most convincing depiction of the symbolic capital of the Fordist aesthetic regime of consumption is in my view not to be found in refined novels or avant-garde cinema, but rather in the rich tradition of satirical Italian comedies. The series of films starring the character of *Fantozzi* shows the misadventures and perpetual unhappiness of a stereotypical Italian white-collar worker, and it remains to this day an unsurpassed grotesque depiction of the alienation of Western post-war consumer society. In the same way, the comedy *Il ragazzo di campagna* ('The country boy') provides an excellent depiction of the symbolic capital of industrial, pop consumption objects. The film – a satirical portrait of Milan during the 1980s, drenched in the myth of progress and wealth – tells the story of a man from the countryside relocating in his 40s to the big city, Milan. In his new house, he receives a call from his mother who wants to send him a parcel full of genuine, traditional food from the farm – a tradition well known today in Italian popular culture as the iconic *pacco da giù* (the *'parcel from Southern Italy'*) and craved by expats from the region. But the country boy of the 1980s, contrary to his contemporary epigones, indignantly refuses and replies that in the city people eat differently, in a more modern and functional way. He then makes himself lunch in an ode to industrial food and pop aesthetic: canned ready-made spaghetti, tinned tuna with a frozen side dish, wine in Tetra Pak packaging; obviously, lunch is then eaten with disposable cutlery, in a disposable dish and glass. The protagonist screams 'This is life!' before starting his banquet. In the next scene, an ambulance brings him to the hospital.

Beyond the satiric metaphor, the pop/kitsch aesthetic regime of consumption offered symbolic capital under the guise of access to a movement toward progress and affluence: the Fordist industrial development. Anyone could leave their rural past behind, and one's previous life, which seemed miserable and undeveloped (what a U-turn compared to today's nostalgia for everything associated with the countryside and the pre-industrial past!) by being part of the ones who were ascending towards a new status and the higher standards of living of the (lower-) middle class. The industrial object exemplified quality and efficiency, and a kitsch aesthetic was perfectly suited to complement its symbolic meaning, providing intrinsic rewards and pleasure through the consumption experience – in a way easily enjoyable by the sociocultural background of the working class. As William Morris foretold at the beginning of the century, the same elite that lamented the despicable destruction of high culture and taste was responsible for that very destruction by playing the role of industrial lords of the kitsch. Still, it is possible to see how kitsch could become an empowering aesthetic for the working class, through its hybridisation with popular culture, even beyond the will of the lords of the kitsch themselves. Building on Walter Benjamin's analysis, Celeste Olalquiaga (1998) developed an original analysis of kitsch's cultural history, positioning its birth – as a phenomenon, not as a term – in the same crucial historical moment of industrialisation and in the sense of loss that it caused during the nineteenth century. Kitsch is what remains of the shattered aura of authenticity embodied by industrial objects. As such, the kitsch aesthetic can be read as consumers' attempt to gain back the intensity and immediacy of consumption in a mechanical era.

When framed in a stereotypical collective imaginary caricaturing its kitschness, the pop aesthetic regime of consumption is the blueprint against which the hip aesthetic regime of consumption builds and reproduces its symbolic power. For hip, authentic consumption to exist, there must always be kitsch consumption as a basis for comparison. Baudrillard noticed it in the *Consumer Society* (2016), stating that 'the kitsch evidently re-values the rare, precious, unique object (whose production can also become industrial). Kitsch and the "authentic" object thus organized the world of consumption by themselves'. The authentic and the kitsch coexist in contemporary consumer society. Not only do they coexist, they continuously hybridise one another in everyday life's processes of consumption.

Sometimes the crossing between the two specular reasonings becomes apparent. For instance, in the fast-fashion model. Hundreds of thousands of standardised, cheap, low-quality clothes are mass-produced in short-lived waves, chasing the ephemeral hip fashion of the moment, to be bought and combined in highly personalised outfits by consumers to express their unique lifestyles. The world of technology is no stranger to this phenomenon, too: the Asian industrious economy produces generally cheap tech products in short-lived and highly distinctive batches to be sold through digital platforms (such as Alibaba), displaying the same combination of aesthetics. Other times, kitsch becomes itself 'hip' thanks to instances of ironic reappropriation, such as the 'camp' aesthetic epitomised by singers and fashion icons such as Cher, Lady Gaga and Katy Perry or by artists like Jeff Koons. More recently, memetic culture – one of the most distinctive cultural phenomena of digital society – marked new heights of kitsch commercial culture re-appropriation and manipulation in extremely sophisticated and hip media artefacts. In the same way as the hip has become paradigmatic of post-Fordist capitalist configuration, there is a drop of kitsch in every authentic consumption experience.

The hip aesthetic regime of consumption substitutes the standardisation of consumer products with the codification of the consumption experience, contradicting the ideal goal of autonomous self-expression and distinctiveness. Becoming paradigmatic in contemporary consumer culture, this process can only naturally converge towards the pop mainstream status it despises, and it is doomed to live with this contradiction. The typical authentic object of consumption may be crafted, but in the vast majority of cases, the hip aesthetic regime of consumption sells industrial, mass-produced objects being given a craft aura thanks to the incessant work of marketing and branding departments. Furthermore, the authentic aura in which objects are presented is partly fictional because it leverages nostalgic, idealised and invented traditions (more on this in the following chapters). The logic of the authentic and of the kitsch co-exist in the same consumption experiences: when killing time on Instagram, we seamlessly evaluate contents and influencers based on their authenticity and at the same time doomscroll cute, kitsch copycat videos of kittens for the immediate pleasurable emotional release that they provide.

A new distinction? Aesthetic regimes of consumption, class and conflict

During the 1990s, sociologist Richard A. Peterson coined the influential notion of 'cultural omnivorousness', arguing the emergence of 'a qualitative shift in the basis for marking elite status – from snobbish exclusion to omnivorous appropriation' (Peterson and Kern, 1996). The wealthy class abandoned the previously typical highbrow taste for a new, composite one, which integrated different styles that it appropriated from the working class. The lowbrow taste, instead, remained confined to being 'univore'.[7] The thesis on cultural omnivorousness became the object of a lively debate, concerning whether the classic division between highbrow and lowbrow taste had become obsolete and sociology should declare the death of highbrow taste, or whether instead this new assumption was deceptive and a marginal phenomenon. Hundreds of articles, chapters and monographs have contributed to this debate up until today, and ultimately many of them converge towards a sort of *new synthesis*, arguing that cultural omnivorousness is indeed a significant consumption phenomenon that, however, has not marked the end of highbrow taste so far, or of any forms of distinction through consumption (see, e.g., Smith Maguire, 2018b; Lizardo and Skiles, 2012; Johnston and Baumann, 2014; Warde *et al.*, 2007).

This book contributes to this new synthesis by more fully interweaving cultural processes in structural economic transformations, traditionally neglected by cultural sociological studies on taste. From this perspective, it could be framed as a first – tentative – formulation of a cultural political economy of taste production and consumption, and as a call for further studies combining these perspectives.[8] By applying the analytical concept of the aesthetic regime of consumption, economic and political factors can be fully appreciated in their interactions with cultural phenomena regarding taste. Such a cultural political economy of taste connects taste with the issues of class, cultural hegemony and conflict.

The pop aesthetic regime of consumption in its Fordist capitalist configuration clearly reveals its intimate bond with a (Western) working class on an upwards social mobility path, looking with hope at a brighter future ahead. It displays a complex, and in equal measure emulating and conflicting, relationship with highbrow taste: it wanted to mimic its conspicuous consumption and aspired to full membership in the new industrial progress, but it also drew from popular culture and was contaminated by it, in an attempt to claim elements of working-class pride and mark a distinction from the bourgeoisie. With the transition from Fordism to post-Fordism, the beneficiaries of Fordism's abundance who joined the middle class – and even more, their educated children – wanted to take a step back from the culture and taste of their youth or of their parents, its alienation and conformity; its social status suddenly seeming vulgar. A hip lifestyle, living and consuming authentically, became a new marker of distinction of an aesthetic regime, which, after the parenthesis of the rampant 1980s and 1990s, gradually became the aesthetic regime of consumption of a middle class living in perennial crisis, stubbornly clinging to it to reaffirm their symbolic capital and social status. Even the hip aesthetic regime of consumption holds a conflictual relationship with both highbrow aesthetics and pop aesthetics' regime of consumption. The latter constituted the negative against which aesthetic values were defined, but at the same time remained a perennial source of appropriation to renew the authenticity and coolness of the aesthetic; the first instead acted as a reference, a benchmark for the quality standard of the consumption experience, and simultaneously as a code for snobbery to be rejected in order to nourish one's own authenticity and alternative status. In simpler terms, the middle class reacted to the crisis by aestheticising popular objects and cultures of consumption, infusing them with high symbolic capital to recreate highly refined but affordable consumption experiences with their precarious economic capital.

Once again, the attempt to capture essential traits of an aesthetic regime of consumption and their relationship with social classes should never translate into an essentialising project or lead to deterministic depictions. Paraphrasing Rousseau and the statements from the previous chapter, there are today as many concrete aesthetics of consumption as there are individuals. The meaning of an aesthetic regime is always fluid, never determined forever or set in stone. A model for the cultural political economy of taste allows the observation of the outcome of a complex array of actors, norms and institutions fighting for the cultural hegemony in a certain time, space and scale. The phenomena of political consumption and consumer resistance have extensively demonstrated the relevance of advancing conflict *through* acts of consumption. The concept of the aesthetic regime of consumption focuses the attention on a different kind of consumer resistance, the one advancing conflict *inside* the field of consumption to establish its hegemonic interpretation. Individuals have been historically recognised as active agents of change in determining the regime of accumulation through their role as workers, and the mode of regulation through their role as citizens: they are equally active agents of change in determining the aesthetic regime of consumption as consumers and taste intermediaries. Picking up, once again, the metaphor of gravity, the more the scale of analysis goes from the macro to the micro, the more the power of consumers becomes visible, and the landscape appears less homogeneous. From this perspective, discussing capitalism's resistance 'against' consumers' agency makes as much sense as discussing consumer resistance against hegemonic aesthetic regimes. After all, this chapter argued that the emergence of a hip aesthetic regime of consumption is tightly linked to consumers expressing their disappointment towards established notions of taste in the streets as well as in the offices of marketing and advertising agencies. The idea of authenticity on which the hip aesthetic regime is built has been appropriated and bridled from a long tradition of thought that, from different perspectives, was born as a tool of resistance against the then paradigmatic aesthetics. This school of thought is indeed still alive, and countless individuals, organisations, small businesses and institutions today use authenticity as the core value around which they establish more or less hybrid aesthetics of consumption.

At the macro level, the new paradigmatic status of a hip aesthetic regime of consumption becomes evident in its power to bend the hegemonic interpretation of the Fordist aesthetic regime of consumption from the 'pop' to the 'kitsch'. From an harbinger of symbolic capital for an upwards looking working class, the display of kitsch aesthetics has become a marker of exclusion from the circle of accultured, 'cool' people – in one word, the 'accomplished' ones. As Bourdieu wrote, the distribution of symbolic capital is the most cruel. The consequence of this new boundary of exclusion between the possessors of hip symbolic capital and the ones who found themselves labelled as 'kitsch' can be seen in every field of society, even in those apparently furthest apart. One example is the political field, where the process of distinction and exclusion of taste contributed to one of the most significant recent phenomena: the so-called 'culture wars' between right-wing populism on the rise among the working-class electorate – who typically live in the countryside and in poorer urban neighbourhoods – against progressive liberalism, embraced instead by educated, urban, middle-class citizens. One of the drivers of the traditional working-class socialist struggle was class hatred against the bourgeoisie; in parallel, one of the drivers of working-class right-wing politics is the hatred against the 'politically correctness' and constant 'virtue signalling' of hip middle-class lifestyles and values. Regardless of the extent to which this image is genuine or fabricated by right-wing, populist neoliberal politicians, this working-class perspective is the consequence of the identification of middle-class aesthetic and values with a new capitalist configuration, which pervasively oppresses them both materially and symbolically.

3
The renaissance of neo-craft industries

In August 2015, McDonald's Ireland launched its first 'artisan burger', the 'McMór' (the literal Gaelic translation of Big Mac). What made it artisanal, in McDonald's eyes, was its recipe composed of ingredients of Irish origin – and in particular the presence of two historical food brands, Ballymaloe relish and Charleville cheddar. The marketing director explained that the company was 'working hard to ensure just the right mix of ingredients to deliver an authentic Irish taste ... in fact, a real taste of home'. Regrettably, the Food Safety Authority of Ireland did not agree. Only one day after the launch of the McMór, the Food Safety Authority of Ireland stated that it did not comply with its guidelines, which allowed food to be labelled as 'artisan' only if it was produced in limited quantities, by skilled craftspeople, not using fully mechanical means and with locally produced ingredients. McDonald's quickly released a piqued note stating it had been made aware that its use of the term artisan was inaccurate, and it would therefore cease to use it. As was to be expected, this event prompted a vast debate in Ireland. In a letter sent to the *Irish Times*, a leading Irish newspaper, a reader presented their perspective: 'Perhaps the Food Safety Authority of Ireland used a sledgehammer to crack a nut. All it had to do was rule that, since the McMór was not being sold at an exorbitant price, it couldn't possibly be classified as artisan.'

McDonald's Ireland's attempt lasted one day, but the overall strategy of the company resisted – and became increasingly refined. In 2017, McDonald's launched a signature series of artisan burgers in the United States, abandoning the project two years later. More recently, in 2022, the company launched the 'Crispy McFillet' in the United Kingdom, made with artisan sourdough bread. At first sight, the idea of McDonald's trying to brand its food as artisan may well seem laughable. McDonald's is a synonym for fast food or junk food, representing the climax of standardised, industrial mass production. Still, the current gravitational power of authenticity as a paradigmatic consumption aesthetic is so strong to bend even McDonald's into adapting to it. In marketing jargon, McDonald's tried to establish a novel brand association to intercept this taste transformation, and it is no surprise that it did so by framing its products as craft. However, the successful application of such a frame proved to be far from an easy operation for McDonald's, as the launch and then abandonment of the signature artisan burgers line in the United States proved. The Food Safety Authority of Ireland based its evaluation on the actual production process, but an even more difficult task is to make the brand association between McDonald's and craft credible in the eyes of the consumers. It is unsurprising that in the end McDonald's seems to have revised its approach to a 'soft strategy', giving up rebranding or launching new product lines directly referring to 'craft' and instead introducing elements connected to notions of typicality, tradition and high-quality products, particularly by using certain ingredients in new specific lines.

As much as craft's symbolic allure may bow the marketing departments of major companies to its will, the comment by the *Irish Times* reader provides a good counterbalance to the picture, illustrating another – more cynical – lens through which the neo-craft phenomenon can be read: a label that allows the strategic sale of overpriced goods for consumption. In this ironic turn of perspective, McDonald's could never be credible in selling 'artisan' food, not because it mostly sells junk food but because of its cheap prices. This observation is both a recurrent belief, to the point of becoming a trope, and simultaneously an apparent paradox. Indeed, one of the most common mockeries towards the stereotypical figure of the hipster in popular culture – and the root of the association with inconsistency and fabrication – is precisely their eagerness to buy overpriced goods for consumption in the neo-craft 'hipster economy'. At the same time, the neo-craft label appeals directly to notions of popular taste and consumption traditions. This chapter will explore the neo-craft phenomenon and related industries by delving into this entanglement of contradicting elements to provide a new theorisation, focusing on the consumption sphere.

The inevitable renaissance of an obsolete mode of production

Today, craft represents the authentic object and process of consumption *par excellence*, even if its obsolescence has been taken for granted for more than a century, with industrialisation and the capitalist mode of production generally considered the culprits (Sennett, 2008). Still, artisans seem to have found their honoured place back in contemporary post-industrial society, particularly in the heart and palate of consumers. Professions such as barmen, barmaids or bartenders, street food vendors, tailors and glassblowers, have all potentially become part of what Chris Land (2018) defines as the 'neo-craft industries': these jobs combine manual work and the preservation of traditional craft imaginary with innovative, skilful manufacturing of high-quality products. They are labelled as 'neo' because they do not embody a simple return to the past. They explicitly refer to the past, or rather to an imaginary, mythicised pre-industrial past, but are well embedded in the post-Fordist, neoliberal economy. In the words of Richard E. Ocejo (2017), neo-craft industries consist of old jobs reinvented and transformed in the new urban economy. Shops, bars and restaurants that are part of the neo-craft industries are the small, cosy venues with characteristically unusual food where one brings their first date, or the pubs with a selection of uncommon craft beers and an unconventional, unique atmosphere for a night out with friends, or again, the hipster bars with a special selection of drinks. In line with the double-faced nature of symbolic capital, they are places chosen for the pleasurable experiences that they provide and for the consecration and reproduction of personal symbolic capital they enable.

In parallel to the high volume of recent academic works discussing the 'quest for authenticity', a proof of the close link between the two phenomena comes from the increasing academic attention to neo-craft entrepreneurs and their paths, narratives and working practises: the PhD research from which this monograph originates is a (modest) example of this tendency. The focus on this topic has good motives. The question of why traditionally working-class jobs suddenly attracted middle-class, highly educated individuals, to the point of pushing them to abandon their occupations – for which they had studied and struggled – to begin a new entrepreneurial venture, surely deserves pondering on. Furthermore, the study of neo-craft entrepreneurs can constitute a privileged viewpoint to contribute to many key debates in contemporary work, such as issues of meaningfulness, ethical entrepreneurship, passionate work, the entrepreneurialisation of work, and authenticity (more on this in the next chapter). Nevertheless, the attention dedicated to the coolness and attractiveness of neo-craft entrepreneurial jobs has neglected one fundamental fact; that the resurgence of the craft economy has been led by consumption, not by production processes. Neo-craft entrepreneurs own small, independent companies. They have certainly further fuelled the growth and rooting in the contemporary urban economy of a hip aesthetic regime of consumption, but their development followed its full blossom in the 1990s, and did not create such popularity. Despite the fact that both neo-craft production and neo-craft consumption are consequences of the post-Fordist will to find an answer to industrial and capitalist alienation through a more authentic life – declined as more meaningful work, on one side; and more meaningful consumption, on the other – the latter has been pivotal in helping neo-craft to burst onto the main stage of the economy. No matter how attractive neo-craft jobs can be, they have flourished and multiplied so extensively in urban landscapes merely thanks to a mass of urban, middle-class consumers just waiting for someone to satisfy their appetites. From this perspective, the historic renaissance of the obsolete craft mode of production seems rather inevitable, led by the new hip aesthetic regime based on authenticity.

Indeed, as the authentic self is the specular reflection of the alienated self, craft as a quality represents the symmetrical opposite of the industrial: small-scale against mass-production, manual against mechanic, creative against dull, skilled against unskilled, unique against serial, distinctive against standardised. The craft object becomes the manifestation of all these properties. Furthermore, the word 'craft' as a verb, beyond the literal meaning, hints at the ultimate outcome of contemporary marketing strategies: experiences tailored around the customer's individuality. On a closer look, craft's renaissance can be read as a by-product of post-Fordism. Almost all the features mentioned above – small-scale production, creativity, skilfulness, personalisation – are also typical of a flexible industrial production and, more recently, of the creative economy. Furthermore, the neo-craft economy follows the same capitalist restructuring led by post-Fordism, shifting the industrious, small-scale economy from the periphery to the centre (Arvidsson, 2019, p. 8). However, craft incarnates these values in their purest form, more than any industrial product could ever do. The manual component and its historic association with the pre-industrial past also allow craft objects to evoke ideas of tradition, typicality and genuineness, particularly in the food and beverage sectors. As further proof of the strong bond between craft and post-Fordism on one side, and the value of authenticity on the other, craft's return to prominence also started in the 1970s and it was led both by developments in the artistic field and by well-explored socio-economic factors: the desire for creative autonomy and self-expression as opposed to consumerism, social conformity and standardised mass-production, through the nostalgia for a romanticised pre-industrial past (Peach, 2013).

Neo-craft or neo-artisan?

Chris Land coined the 'neo-craft' label to clarify that this new renaissance of craft is a post-industrial and post-Fordist phenomenon, whose relationship to neoliberalism is at best ambivalent. There are other good reasons to distinguish 'neo-craft' industries from what can be summarily defined as 'old crafts'. From a commercial point of view, craft beer leads the neo-craft economy thanks to its staggering success, which has reshaped the entire beer sector. Estimates of craft beer's global market value can differ significantly, but in general they amount to many dozens of billion dollars. From a consumer perspective, the most pervasive and visible neo-craft industry is the food and beverage sector in general, especially in urban retailing contexts: restaurants, bars, pubs, cafés but also independent grocery stores, butcher stores, delis, winehouses, and the likes. If William Morris was reborn to see the neo-craft industries that are carrying on his old dreams and values in the new millennium, there is a good chance that he would be at first bewildered, if not upset. The arts and crafts to which he referred were actually decorative arts: jewellery, pottery, metalwork, leatherwork, shoemaking, glassblowing and fashion. He spoke of functional objects, generally durable, with extraordinary quality and displayed mastery. The vast majority of existing organisations representing craft producers in different geographic contexts still shares the same considerations. From this viewpoint, neo-craft goods seem too ephemeral to belong to the same category. Indeed, recent books for the general public either lamented the exclusion of craft beer from craft professions as an injustice (Brown, 2020), or criticised the rise of craft beer as an abuse of the 'craft' label for mere marketing purposes (Langlands, 2017). Whether victims of unfair exclusion or nefarious marketing tools, one thing is certain; the symbolic leaders of neo-craft industries are the pretenders, or the parvenu, of the craft landscape.

The first explanation for this complex landscape emerges when taking into account the cultural context of the words being used. Craft originates from old English and has maintained in modern history the aforementioned strong association with decorative arts (Adamson, 2018). Artisan, instead, is a word of Italian and French origin. According to the *Oxford English Dictionary*, the craftsperson is 'a person who is skilled at a particular craft; a worker in a skilled trade; an artisan'. The artisan, instead, is 'a worker in a skilled trade, a craftsperson; (in later use) esp. one utilizing traditional or non-mechanized methods'. The latter definition hints at a recent broadening of meaning: artisan can refer to anyone using traditional or non-mechanised methods, regardless of whether they work in a traditionally established craft or not. This shift seems to reflect a degree of French and Italian contextual influence. In both national contexts, the artisan is an officially recognised professional category including very different skills: craftspeople are considered together with electricians, plumbers, car mechanics *and* workers in the food industry, making it much easier for bakers, butchers, cooks and similar professionals to define themselves through the status of artisans. The French organisations that are part of the World Craft Council Europe, which, as previously illustrated, follows the traditional definition of craft of British origin, refers to its members as the professionals practising 'artistic crafts' in English, or *artisans d'art* or *métiers d'art* in French, to clearly distinguish them from the broader artisan category. The craft label in the Anglo-American context progressively incorporated this more extensive meaning. According to the *Oxford English Dictionary*, the definition of craft includes 'later also more generally: any activity involving making things by hand or by means of traditional techniques'.

A matter of petty conspicuous consumption

From the above discussion, it could be argued that the neo-craft industries are actually led by neo-artisans. Still, the idea of craft influences neo-artisans as well, blending the two ideas: they want to manipulate objects in traditional or non-mechanical ways and to apply the standards of quality and mastery usually attributed to artistic crafts to their more ephemeral objects of consumption, only in a different way. The same is valid for consumers: they appreciate the symbolic qualities of crafts attached to objects of their daily consumption. Elizabeth Currid-Halkett (2017) in the *Sum of the Small Things* explains how the new middle class – in comparison to the older one – seeks 'inconspicuous consumption' to demonstrate their social status through the possession of exclusive cultural sophistication rather than economic capital, due to the popularisation and growing accessibility of material – and even luxury – goods. A few years before, Douglas McWilliams (2015) in the *Flat White Economy* offered a slightly more prosaic motivation when describing the impressive growth of hipster businesses in London. Unlike the middle class employed in the rampant pre-crisis economy of the 1980s and 1990s, its contemporary counterpart has social prestige but can no longer afford supercars and champagne: only cool bicycles, flat-white coffees and craft beers.

Both interpretations capture one side of the significant appeal of craft products. The legitimate consumption of craft products requires high levels of cultural sophistication (i.e., the knowledge and ability to appreciate a hip aesthetic regime of authenticity), which allows such products to remain a source of distinction. Still, despite the widespread mockery of hipsters, craft products are offered at prices pertaining to a different, lower category when compared to luxury products. If their consumption has become inconspicuous, it is at least partially to make a virtue out of necessity. The characteristic neo-craft consumption of organic groceries, typical food plates, signature cocktails, fancy bikes, distinctive clothing, authentic tourist experiences *et similia* seems to accurately describe a new category of 'petty conspicuous consumption', fitting perfectly the purposes of a new middle class who lives in an age of perennial crisis and precariousness. The possession of an abundance of cultural capital but lagging wealth precludes the access to previously standard markers of conspicuous consumption such as large houses, expensive cars and luxury goods, among others.

The attitude of petty conspicuous consumption characterising the ideal-typical consumers of neo-craft products helps to explain why objects of consumption from the food and beverage sector gained such prominence in neo-craft industries: they allow distinctiveness and authentic consumption experiences at affordable prices. By being objects of ephemeral, direct consumption, foods and drinks satisfy the contemporary consumer's quest for authenticity through experiential pleasure, a model of 'liquid consumption' (Bardhi and Eckhardt, 2017) particularly predominant in the digital sphere. To the same extent, as already argued, the neo-craft renaissance has been led by a transformation in the consumption sphere, and not by technical improvements in craft production. From the point of view of time and cost efficiency, industrial production maintains the same comparative advantage against handcrafted manufacturing that led to the rise of the industrial society and to the success of the Fordist capitalist configuration.[1] However, the difference between industrial and handcrafted products is not the same for every industry. Furnishing a new house with pieces entirely crafted by a master carpenter is on a different scale of costs than going to IKEA, and the same applies to the choice between only wearing sartorial clothes compared to buying retail clothes. Since they are ephemeral objects of everyday consumption, food and beverages have baseline costs that make it easier for consumers to pay the craft surcharge, still taking advantage of the acquisition or reproduction of the symbolic capital associated with the authentic craft consumption experience. They allow, once again, 'petty forms of conspicuous consumption' that would otherwise be economically out of reach, thanks to their craft symbolic overload and overexposure. This also means that traditional craft professions are not necessarily excluded from neo-craft industries, they simply usually play a less visible role.

The craft and the crafty

As the opening example of the McMór exemplified, self-declared craft or artisan commodities flood the contemporary consumer society well beyond the perimeter of small and independent neo-craft producers. If the attempt by McDonald's can be dismissed as a clumsy marketing action, due to the discrepancy between the brand in question and the craft imaginary, this is not always the case. The first industry to realise this has been the craft beer sector, which leads the neo-craft phenomenon in terms of market size. Already in 2012, the American Brewers Association – whose goal is 'to promote and protect craft brewers, their beers, and the community of brewers enthusiasts' (Brewers Association, 2022) – released a press statement (Brewers Association, 2012) alarmed by the fact that 'the large brewers have been seeking entry into the craft beer marketplace. Many started producing their own craft-imitating beers, while some purchased (or are attempting to purchase) large or full stakes in small and independent breweries'. This would not be a problem, they continued, if it wasn't for the fact that 'the large, multinational brewers appear to be deliberately attempting to blur the lines between their crafty, craft-like beers and true craft beers from today's small and independent brewers'.

Their fear was justified: for someone outside the narrow circle of beer connoisseurs, it is indeed a very tricky task to distinguish between craft and 'crafty' beers just by looking at the supermarket shelf or the pub's beer taps. Beer labels such as the Blue Moon or Goose Island brand themselves as 'craft' despite being owned by multinational companies. A savvy combination of factors concurs to confuse consumers: the design of the logo, the can or bottle, in a unique and alternative style; the use of labels such as IPA or APA; the removal of any explicit reference to the parent company. In most cases, these companies' goal is to attach as many craft attributes as possible to their beers, knowing that a partial craft appeal – no matter how artificial – is still better than no craft appeal at all. One example is the most successful case of crafty beer in the Italian market, the 'unfiltered Ichnusa'. Despite having a long history as a standard industrial beer, the Heineken group (who owns the brand) has built on the regional bond of the 'Ichnusa' beer with the region of Sardinia to launch a new product line with strong craft allure. The key elements of this operation, besides the will to reinforce the link with Sardinia, are the fact that the beer is unfiltered – instinctively associated with craft brewing methods – and a distinctive bottle design and format (50 cl, like a pub's pint, usually reserved for cans). Obviously, the beer is still industrially produced, and most consumers somehow know it, but the partial craft attributes and slight distinctiveness from other beers still made it a favourite on pubs' taps and supermarket shelves.

The case of craft beer is emblematic, but a similar set of examples could be drawn from the food industry, and more in general from all the industries interested in craft production. All in all, the corporate strategic appropriation of the 'craft' quality from small and independent craftspeople is a natural consequence of the co-optation of the ideal of authenticity from countercultures analysed in the last chapter and appears to be in line with a long tradition of capitalist co-optations. Craft historian Sandra Alfoldy, following this line of thought, defined this process as 'craftwashing' – in a book unfortunately left unpublished due to her premature death. In the posthumous article *Crafting Kindness*, she illustrates an instance of craftwashing using the example of a meeting with one of her students:

> And there I was, standing in front of one of my undergraduate students, struggling to differentiate between the mug she'd carefully handcrafted and the one she'd bought at IKEA. The poor young woman was almost distraught. Her mug would have to sell for over $40.00 in order to recoup her materials and labour, but the one she'd purchased for under $10.00 from a multinational corporation? How could she compete? . . . what both she and I could not get over was not only how well-crafted the corporate mug appeared, but how well-craft-branded it was. The label had its own handcrafted aesthetic and was attached with a raffia ribbon (a sure sign of kindness and careful craftsmanship!), and rather than promising the consumer that it was made by an individual craftsperson, it used the term 'carefully designed.' Where? By whom? And who actually made it? (Alfoldy, 2018, p. 179)

For Alfoldy, craftwashing mirrors the kindness intrinsic in craft and reproduces simulacra of the affective qualities of craft, thereby tricking consumers. However, by scratching the surface we find that the tension between neo-craft and crafty commodities is not – just – a matter of multinationals deceiving ingenuous consumers. Indeed, consumers in this situation seem to be fooled to the extent to which they decide to play along and participate in this game of disguise: they know that the emperor is naked, that the majority of commodities – especially in mass-market retailing – is industrially produced and just rebranded as craft, but they buy them anyway because, when manufactured according to some minimum canons, these products still present a more preferable outlook than blunt industrial commodities without concealment. The commercial success of commodities that are overtly crafty (i.e., that do not hide their industrial nature but mimic craft products) in all major retailing industries prove the truth behind the provocation opening this monograph: most of us are all a little bit hipster(ist) when we consume; we look for properties attributable to craft ideals in objects of consumption, and we tend to choose the ones that accumulate more of these properties with a credible general craft claim.

The intensity with which craft attributes orient our consumption choices and our degree of satisfaction with the credibility of the claim vary from one individual to the next, but also depend on the situation: people resembling more closely the hipster subculture, will maintain stricter standards; consumers with strong political conscience or deeply involved in food or drinking cultures could hold different evaluation criteria; other consumers – as the reader of the *Irish Times* – may reject products adhering to craft ideals by principle, or embrace hybrid crafty products instead. In the same way, we set the bar differently depending on whether we buy groceries at the supermarket or at a local market, or have dinner with relatives rather than with friends. Just like in the metaphor of gravity, the pull towards craft consumption is a gravitational force: at the level of micro-interactions, a massive number of other variables intervene – more decisively – in the consumption process. At the same time, the ability to appreciate the difference between craft and crafty products becomes a new mark of distinction between a cultivated middle class and an unsophisticated, lowbrow class.

The aura of craft objects and the neo-craft economic imaginary

Even though the difference between neo-craft and a crafty may seem intuitive, what constitutes a neo-craft object of consumption remains unclear. A handcrafted mug worked by a potter, like in the example by Alfoldy, is intuitively identified as a neo-craft object. But what about a cocktail prepared by a mixologist in a cool bar, or street food served by a gourmet food truck at a festival? Where do we draw the line between neo-craft and crafty products in similar situations? These questions were frequently a source of worry for the bar owners and food truck vendors that I interviewed. Starting from the assumption that they were authentic neo-artisans (of course), they frequently discussed sincere and 'dishonest' colleagues, a discussion further compounded by the difficulty of defining themselves as professionals and distinguishing themselves from more traditional retailers. Some of them were planning to create a recognised association, gathering all the legitimate neo-artisans in the sector. Still, this proposal has clear drawbacks: the definition of who is a reputable neo-artisan and who is not is subjective and the two categories may seem to overlap. To better understand the distinction between neo-craft, crafty and traditional craft products, it is necessary to analyse the symbolic meaning evoked by the neo-craft label. Answering this question also allows us to clarify the relationship – to an extent still foggy – between neo-craft as a consumption phenomenon and the paradigmatic hip aesthetic regime of consumption. This journey to the symbolic meaning of neo-craft requires two new concepts: the concept of economic imaginaries of consumption and that of aura.

I draw the concept of the economic imaginary of consumption mainly from two theorisations: the cultural political economy approach by Ngai-Ling Sum and Bob Jessop (2013) and Jens Beckert's (2016) theory of economic imaginaries. Inspired by Michel Foucault's and Antonio Gramsci's reading of political economy (Sum, 2009), the cultural political economy approach conceptualises 'economic imaginaries' as narrative-coherent complexes that give meaning to a set of otherwise unintelligible economic transactions, shaping the economic field itself. Economic ideas are 'a constitutive force in shaping economic forms and relations' (Jessop, 2009), and the formalisation of economic imaginaries is a highly discretionary operation, which – deliberately or not – highlights some features and hides others. This theorisation is a useful reminder of the fact that economic phenomena never reach society as a neutral label, but rather as a performative force. Economic imaginaries can be powerful gears in the reproduction system of a specific capitalist configuration, bound to regimes of accumulation, reproduction and consumption (or, more rarely, powerful instruments of critique to a capitalist configuration). Discussing the return of 'neo-craft economy' means referring to a specific economic imaginary, linked to the developments of a hip aesthetic regime of consumption, harnessed from its origin by the macro post-Fordist capitalist configuration and adopted by neo-craft micro-entrepreneurs to envision post-industrial, sometimes even post-neoliberal alternatives. In this semantic ambiguity, the neo-craft economy becomes a battlefield for cultural hegemony.

The cultural political economy approach firmly situates economic imaginaries in the macro-realm of capitalist reproduction, but shows its weakness when explaining how such an economic imaginary of consumption intersects with the micro level of everyday interaction populated by consumers. Here is where Beckert's theory of imagined futures comes in handy to 'discern the micro-foundations of macro-economic processes' (Beckert, 2016, p. 8). Economic imaginaries of consumption according to Beckert play a fundamental role in organising the fictional expectations of consumers towards a commodity in two main ways. First, they help consumers to deal with the uncertainty associated with any consumption choice, allowing them to project upon a commodity the satisfaction of specific expectations and desires. By choosing a commodity associated with the neo-craft imaginary, individuals expect that their desire for an authentic consumption experience will be satisfied. Second, economic imaginaries of consumption allow individuals to attach a symbolic meaning to commodities beyond their material qualities, with a bounded agency: they can play with different imaginaries, but these come pre-packaged. This brings us back to the inescapable necessity to link the macro and the micro level, by recognising that 'the production of consumer dreams is itself a productive force in the economy' (p. 191). Furthermore, by combining Beckert's theory with Bourdieu's notion of symbolic capital analysed in the previous chapter, it becomes apparent that the symbolic value of commodities presents the same double-edged nature: it is both positional, as it provides the consumer with social reputation deriving from the societal evaluation of the commodity, and imaginative, as it provides intrinsic pleasure deriving from the intimate relationship between the consumer and the commodity. The neo-craft economic imaginary of consumption enables intimate, pleasurable, authentic experiences *and* petty conspicuous consumption in society. Lastly, economic imaginaries of consumption develop in four dimensions:

> The imaginary power of consumer goods occurs in several dimensions: it occurs through time, by associating their owners with a desired future state or a distant past; through space, by connecting their owners to desired but distant or unreachable places; socially, by linking their owners to out-of-reach people; and through values, by linking their owners to values they espouse. (p. 195)

This scheme proves useful in order to present 'neo-craft' as an economic imaginary of consumption. From a temporal point of view, neo-craft consumer goods represent a movement 'back to the future': to quote Land (2018), they refer to an idealised pre-industrial past to envision meaningful and pleasurable post-industrial futures. From a space perspective, the neo-craft goods allow their generally urban consumers trapped in contemporary city life to perform a symbolic move back to the countryside,[2] to genuine ingredients, simple pleasures, contemplative relationship with nature; in one word, 'authentic' experiences, far from anything industrial. These goods also allow consumers to discover and bond with ingredients, products and traditions from distant cultures in a (supposedly) authentic way. Through a social lens, entering the neo-craft economic imaginary as a consumer means stating one's refined taste for the authentic, which ideally enables the access to a cosmopolitan social class of fellow consumers characterised by a certain symbolic capital – the one that Ocejo (2017) summarises as the 'coolness' of neo-craft industries. This leads us to the last dimension: values. The ability of the neo-craft economic imaginary of consumption to transmit the quality of 'craft' to commodities relies on several values, which can be employed in a variety of combinations: tradition, typicality, genuineness, artistic quality, materiality, intimacy with nature, sustainability and uniqueness. These values are also essential in connecting the economic imaginary to the broader aesthetic regime of consumption.

Indeed, the economic imaginaries of consumption can be fully understood only in their connection with the aesthetic regimes of consumption. They translate the taste paradigms operating at the macro, gravitational level of capitalist configurations in the micro-realm of economic interactions between producers, consumers and intermediaries. They provide an operationalisation of the overarching – and more abstract – taste principles (i.e., the desire for authenticity and the refusal of anything industrial) into a set of qualities and values more directly recognisable for consumers and applicable to commodities. It might not be immediately clear what constitutes 'authentic' food, but the concept of artisanal food gives a much clearer mental image: quality food made with typical ingredients from a region, following traditional recipes, etc.

The revival of the craft as a phenomenon can be considered a consequence of the rise of a neo-craft economic imaginary of consumption, which in turn is connected to the general aesthetic regime of consumption based on authenticity. Neo-craft objects of consumption legitimately embody such an economic imaginary, letting consumers experience its related dimensions during the consumption act. But how does this process of embodiment and experience work? To find this out, a theorisation of aura and auratic perception, inspired by Walter Benjamin, proves useful. Benjamin discusses the notion of aura in multiple works, with conflicting theorisations (Duttlinger, 2008). Still, some core features can be drawn (Leslie, 2000).

First, auratic perception is necessarily a relational and experiential phenomenon. The aura acts as a medium, whereby the subject and the object encounter and experience unity. In other words, the attribution of an aura to an object is a social relation, rather than an intrinsic property. Second, auratic perception is not immediate, but rather, in order to be appreciated, the aura has to respond to certain societal norms and interpretive canons hidden from the first perception. Third, the aura is neither a necessary feature of objects nor a 'neutral' experience. For Benjamin, auratic perception corresponds to a positive state of contemplation, affirmation of one's own individuality, and authenticity. Technological and social developments caused by industrialisation led to a decline in experiences of auratic perceptions. At the same time, industrial capitalism permeated society with a fake, artificial aura, applied to standardised mass-produced products. The artificial aura is formulaic, erasing the interpretive distance between the consumer and the object of consumption through the use of a kitsch aesthetic and favouring the commodification of the self.

Considering objects of consumption through the conceptualisation of aura enables us to recognise that the neo-craft attribute has a fundamental symbolic nature. Neo-craft objects of consumption display a legitimate neo-craft aura; they embody the neo-craft economic imaginary of consumption in a way that is recognisable by consumers. Given that aura is a relational quality, the legitimacy of the auratic perception of the commodity varies according to the consumers. Benjamin's dualism between 'authentic' and 'fake' auras also provides further substantiation to the relationship between neo-craft and crafty commodities. Even if both neo-craft and crafty commodities can be considered artificial, since they both attempt to create a craft aura from scratch, there are some pivotal differences. For neo-craft, middle-class entrepreneurs, led by the aspiration of achieving an authentic life through artisanal practises, the goal of recovering the neo-craft aura serves the purpose of recreating the same auratic perception of pre-industrial consumption objects. In the production of crafty commodities, instead, the link to the economic imaginary aims at forcefully attaching a mimicked aura to industrial objects of consumption, artificially intercepting the taste for the authentic. The symbolic and ethical components disappear, and the entire operation acquires a predominantly economic goal.

The neo-craft economy and crafty capitalism

Further stressing the craft/crafty dualism, and recalling the fundamental Braudelian distinction (Braudel, 1977) between the market economy – the layer of horizontal economic relations of competition and cooperation between small enterprises and of small profits – and the capitalist economy – the top layer of oligopolies and big capitals accumulation – the industrious neo-craft economy and crafty capitalism can be further exposed as two different entrepreneurial logics. These logics find their roots in the contemporary neo-craft economic imaginary of consumption, which shows the same fundamental ambiguity: authenticity is at the core of both countercultural projects of emancipation from alienation and hegemonic projects of further consumers' commodification. The distinction between these two logics often implies an opposition, with small producers claiming their alternative nature in comparison to the capitalist corporations exploiting the neo-craft trend for marketing purposes, but it is not clear-cut. Reality – as often happens – is a puzzle rich of grey zones and hybrid contaminations. For example, to assume that every product manufactured by a small and independent neo-artisan is naturally neo-craft would be a mischievous assumption.

The crafty nature of an object can be concealed in the case of small and independent retailers or producers, too, and despite some common agreement, the boundaries are fluid. For example, almost all the neo-artisans that I interviewed agreed on one category that they considered an expression of crafty, capitalist logic: those colleagues simply selling fried food. Why? Because, as an old southern Italian adage says, 'Even a shoe's sole becomes tasty when you fry it'. Frying standardises the taste of food, and it means the care put into the choice of the ingredients becomes superfluous – and even useless. Fried food is also a typical feature of southern Italy's popular cuisine. This way, small entrepreneurs with a capitalist logic could just mimic the others' design, buy industrial food from mass-market retailers, deep-fry it on their truck, brand it as authentic by serving it in a Neapolitan *cuoppo* (a cone of wax paper) or equivalent, and sell it as typical street food from Italian tradition. Interestingly, the example of 'crafty' fryers also creates an interesting paradox and exposes some contradictions in neo-artisan industries.

Fried food is typical of popular, working-class tradition *precisely* because it allows taste to be standardised, making second-rate food (the proverbial 'sole' of the shoe) more tasty; but this feature becomes a malus when demonstrating legitimate membership to neo-craft industries, that now respond to a middle-class aesthetics of consumption.

4
The neo-craft micro-entrepreneurs

From Sartre onwards, jazz has been considered the authentic musical form of expression *par excellence*. In the documentary '*Monk, Pannonica: Une histoire américaine*', dedicated to the legendary jazz musician Thelonious Monk, a commentator argued that 'every jazz musician wants to play in a totally unique way, write the songs that everyone wants to play, and at the same time to progress the entire genre'. The same can be said for the neo-craft entrepreneurs: they want to express themselves in a totally unique way, create the neo-craft commodities everyone wants to consume, and contribute to progressing the entire neo-craft movement with its values. Neo-craft entrepreneurs constitute the engine of the neo-craft industries, a new wave of individuals fuelling the neo-craft imaginary and satisfying the taste for authenticity of consumers. At the same time, they also are meso level actors in the process of taste formation. From this premise, the present chapter will develop an analysis of the identity, work experience and role of cultural intermediaries of neo-craft entrepreneurs. This chapter heavily relies on the empirical findings gathered during my doctoral path, for which I interviewed 40 neo-craft owners of gourmet food trucks, bars and restaurants in the city of Milan between 2017 and 2019. The occasional quotes, except for when differently specified, will come from their accounts and have been translated by me.[1]

A peculiar kind of entrepreneurial self

The neo-craft industries are a post-Fordist phenomenon embedded in the context of neoliberalism. One pillar of neoliberalism, derived from what Luc Boltanski and Eve Chiapello (2007) would define as the incorporation of the artistic critique to Fordism, has been individualism: the exaltation of individual freedom, creativity and self-expression. Individualism has deep roots as well, which partially plunge into the same Romantic environment so fundamental for the development of the idea of authenticity (Lukes, 2006). Still, neoliberalism has oriented individualism in a very precise direction: towards the entrepreneurial self (Brockling, 2015). On this path, the imperative is to exclusively think of the self as a marketplace agent, and of freedom and self-expression as something to be exercised in purely economic terms. This phenomenon is so strong that even employee work growingly responds to the laws, criteria and expectations of entrepreneurial work (Neff, 2013). Still, as all the phenomena analysed up until now, even the process of entrepreneurialisation of the self presents some ambiguities. Capitalism's structural power guides but does not determine the process, and it always leaves room for alternative uses of the same trends. As the Italian author Sergio Bologna (2018) argued through historical analyses, the 'rise of the European self-employed workforce' was also led by workers greeting autonomous work and micro-entrepreneurship as the perfect opportunity to free themselves from salaried work and the alienation of Fordist society. Embracing autonomous work was also a political choice, part of the broader planning of alternative life projects guided by the search for authenticity, meaningfulness and pleasure common among the members of the protest movements of the 1960s and 1970s. Bologna pictures an illustrative fresco of the complex set of motivations leading this wave of new workforce:

> Those that had become complacent, those that had thrown in the towel ('let's get rich!'), those who – not having succeeded in eliminating their bosses – wanted at least in their personal life to not have one . . . and those, perhaps the majority, who believed they had developed, thanks to their 'out of the ordinary' political and organizational experiences, some special people-handling skills. (Bologna, 2018, p. 62)

It is known in history that, despite the intention of these freelance pioneers, the neoliberal logic of the entrepreneurialised self (particularly in the 1980s and 1990s) wiped out any possibility of hegemonic countercultural politicisations of autonomous work.[2] Still, as argued in the introduction, the recent global economic crisis and the corresponding multiple signals for the failure of neoliberalism have opened the door to a second wave self-employed workforce using entrepreneurial work for more-than-economic goals. As Adam Arvidsson argues, for the contemporary industrious economy:

> Entrepreneurship is not simply something that is hammered into the heads of young by teachers, social workers and career counsellors. It is also something that is embraced by a large number of people, a far larger number, arguably, than those who still engage in politics in the classic, twentieth-century sense of the term. For these people, entrepreneurship is not simply an economic activity. It also comes for a vision of social transformation . . . It has taken over from politics as the main field in which such action can unfold in the pragmatic everyday of 'actually doing something'. (Arvidsson, 2019, p. 11)

The neo-craft entrepreneurs fit perfectly into the above descriptions. Just like their progenitors in the 1970s, they embraced entrepreneurship as part of wider alternative life projects. Unlike their progenitors, however, neo-craft entrepreneurs are children of the post-Fordist neoliberal economy. In this regard, they share many features with the most renowned entrepreneurial figure of post-Fordism: the creative start-uppers of the digital economy. Both are characterised by the fact that they embraced autonomous work to escape the alienation of corporate jobs, searching for meaning and personal fulfilment inside work, blurring between working and personal time, putting to work the cultural and symbolic capital at their disposal, and enjoying non-monetary rewards. Both can be said to adhere to the model of the entrepreneurialised self, conceiving political action as something to perform through market agency, as exemplified by the majestic social missions declared by the most influential Silicon Valley tycoons: they want to connect the entire world digitally, save humanity by going to Mars, create a global metaverse, etc.

However, neo-craft entrepreneurs are also different compared to their more celebrated relatives in many relevant aspects. Most evident is that, unlike the founders of high-tech companies, their jobs are labour-intensive and have low requirements in terms of capital. Start-ups may be launched with tiny amounts of seed capital by relatives or business angels, but to fulfil their ambitious promises they must go 'from zero to one'. And there is only one way to reach 'one': accumulate massive amounts of (venture) capital from investors.

Neo-craft entrepreneurs, instead, want to open a shop, a food truck or a restaurant: if anything, their aim is to expand at the local level, opening one or more branches. They will never become – and generally do not even want to become – the next Mark Zuckerberg or the next Uber. They do not aspire to attract $1 billion in private equity capital because they would not know what to do with the money (for their businesses, at least). They do not intend to revolutionise humankind through their disruptive technology or to colonise Mars. Instead, they wish to play their part in a bigger movement of small enterprises promoting specific ethical values and making the world a better place, one sandwich or cocktail at a time.

If start-uppers are betting on the promise of the creative economy to reach wealth and fame, neo-craft entrepreneurs seem to have already given up on that gamble. They traded the dream of becoming a member of the 'new economic elite' for the possibility of reaching ethical gratification, with authenticity becoming the currency of exchange enabling the process of detachment from the material, economic rewards of entrepreneurship. They constitute a hybrid model of the entrepreneurial self, in which non-economic goals become prevalent. Emulating the Marxian general formula of capital, Michael Scott (2017) summarised this process as 'CC-EC-CC[E]': the use of limited economic capital (EC) to build on an initial cultural capital (CC) and reach cultural success together with economic benefits. Still, when analysing the neo-craft imaginary, the exclusive focus on cultural capital seems partially misleading. The goal of neo-craft entrepreneurs is first and foremost the achievement of symbolic capital and social and political change.

The rise of such a peculiar and alternative form of entrepreneurialised self mirrors the rise of 'woke capitalism' (Rhodes, 2021), the recent trend – which is also a necessity – previously analysed in corporations to growingly brand themselves as responsible companies, addressing tangible social issues or rectifying their past wrongdoings. Still, as in the comparison between the neo-craft economy and crafty capitalism advanced in the previous chapter, neo-craft micro-entrepreneurs – who obviously cannot compete with corporations on the level of scale – are naturally advantaged when it comes instead to convincing consumers of the authenticity of their commitment, as even the most committed corporations such as apparel brand Patagonia can be met with controversies and criticisms. Neo-craft entrepreneurs remain small, with very short supply chains and without the pressure to quickly scale up or die, and therefore can easily stay consistent with their ethical goals.

The neo-craft entrepreneurs' identity

The German sociologist Hans Speier, observing the Weimer Republic after the Great Regression, noticed that the self-employed workforce was a class without identity (Bologna, 2018). The combined effect of the crisis on one side and the rise of Fordism on the other made self-employed workers a category about to disappear, having lost their identity and social prestige. The contemporary neo-craft entrepreneurs could be conceived as protagonists of an opposite status: they are a rising force in the industrious economy of contemporary society. If the self-employed workforce of the 1930s had lost their identity, the neo-craft entrepreneurs seem to have not yet formed one: they lack a unanimous definition in terms of class and occupational identity. All the entrepreneurs that I interviewed expressed this very clearly. They were reluctant to be defined as 'artisans' themselves, but seemed to accept that their work can be considered artisanal, to mark the distinction from traditional retailers. They consider artisanal labour to be composed of the inextricable co-existence of the creative and manual dimension. The artisanal working act, in which the freely expressed intellectual endeavour shapes the manual act, and in turn the manual act provides a special relationship with materials and a sense of meaning, is a fundamental source of gratification.

When it came to defining themselves, these interviewees responded with great variety: apart from some classic answers such as entrepreneurs, cooks or bartenders, a lot of different, often eclectic self-definitions were provided. Even when classic labels were mentioned, such as 'bartender', it often came with some degree of dissatisfaction with the definition, deemed unable to capture their profession's specificity: 'I call myself a bartender [*barista* in Italian] even though today, when saying bartender, we tend to include many different professions, actually' (Claudio, bar owner). In other cases, they revived occupations rooted in Italian tradition, like the one of *oste* or of *salumiere* (which translate roughly to 'innkeeper' and 'butcher', respectively) but felt uneasy using such humble terms in the context of refined cocktail bars or gourmet restaurants: 'On my Facebook profile, I defined myself as an innkeeper ['*oste*' in Italian] . . . obviously it is a bit of a joke. But since I like talking to people, hearing their stories' (Tina, bar owner). The difficulty with these peculiar, ill-fitting identities is acknowledged, but the names are still sometimes used for personal satisfaction. This general unease sometimes brought to a simple refusal of providing an occupational definition, a request perceived as impossible and degrading, a forcing into pre-established categories:

> I would call myself a 'pucciologist' [in Italian 'pucciologo', a wordplay based on *puccia*, a special bread from Salento, and -ologo, the suffix indicating an expert in a specific field], but I cannot. I consider myself a creative explosion that reinvents itself every time, how else could I define myself. (Brando, food truck owner)

Beside the recent development of the neo-craft industries, it is easy to recognise other causes at the root of this plethora of colourful definitions. First, the necessity to mark a difference from the broader occupational category to which these professionals formally pertain, but with which they have little in common. Neo-craft bar owners are bartenders, but of a very peculiar kind. Gourmet food truck owners are itinerant street food sellers, but again, of a very peculiar kind. What differentiates them is not some objective criterion that can be included in an industry definition. Indeed, the neo-craft industries are defined by the adherence to a symbolic economic imaginary of consumption, and it becomes extremely personalised. This means that once the distinction from their traditional colleagues is set, it becomes very difficult to find a clear-cut, broad occupational definition that can be applied beyond the individual. The second dimension has precisely to do with individuality. Indeed, neo-craft entrepreneurs tend to individualise their identities in a very distinctive, unique way. The 'antifascist bartender', the *cocinero*, and the 'pusher of taste' are some examples from my interviews. This tailoring of a unique identity is an outcome of both their hybrid entrepreneurial self, which valorises individualism, and of the symbolic dimension they embrace, which is connected to authenticity and obviously emphasises forms of unique self-expression, personal creativity and distinctiveness. Furthermore, the development of a unique identity signals the presence of a hip symbolic capital and reinforces the legitimate membership to the neo-craft economic imaginary. Lastly, it is a strategic action for economic goals, reached by carving out a unique, highly recognisable identity.

A tripartite model of neo-craft entrepreneurial ideal types

The narratives employed by neo-craft entrepreneurs about the motivation guiding them and steering their identities revolve around a stable set of values, deeply rooted in ethics: passion towards one's job, self-expression, artisanship, authenticity, creativity and innovation. They genuinely embrace them, but are also aware of the fact that these same values are an essential requirement to be a successful entrepreneur in the hipster economy. These two aspects are not in contrast but, rather, are complementary, mirroring the double function of symbolic capital as a source of external and internal goods (Banks, 2017); that is, respectively economic reward with social prestige and intrinsic pleasure. Self-sustenance and self-realisation always come in pairs, and their inextricable co-occurrence is a key feature of identity-making in the neo-craft economic imaginary. Similarly, another tension characterises neo-craft entrepreneurs' identity: it is both an expression of mastery and slavery (Butler, 1997). It is mastery, because their adhesion to the economic imaginary marks their status as skilful users and manipulators of the concepts and values of the imaginary. But it is also slavery, because they contextually decide to submit their fundamental set of values and qualities to an imaginary that they are free to use, but not to alter. The values that allow them to express their agency are the very same values that also limit it. The neo-craft economic imaginary of consumption exerts on its entrepreneurs a process of 'creative governmentalisation' (Banks, 2017, p. 92), promoting their artistic and creative freedom while regulating their identities at the same time. The empowerment deriving from the freedom to express one's true self and to determine one's own professional subjectivity is granted at the cost of the implicit conformity to the canons and the boundaries of the imaginary, in a new codification of legitimate aesthetics.

The already presented peculiar kind of entrepreneurialised self and the tension between contrasting pressures contribute to the inherent difficulty in finding a collective, shared definition to express their identity from an occupational point of view. The fragmentation of the identity claims does not prevent, however, the identification of recurrent patterns among neo-craft entrepreneurs, leading to a categorisation into three ideal types. To accomplish this task, I took inspiration from Collinson's (2003) analysis of 'subjectivities at work' under surveillance-based organisations, which distinguishes between 'conformists', 'dramaturgical' and 'resistant' employees. Translated to the context of the neo-craft industries, surveillance-based management is the economic imaginary of consumption, and individuals are micro-entrepreneurs, not employees. This implies that the power relation is not strictly unidirectional (the organisation exerts power on the employees, that can only comply with the instructions or try to resist) but partially bi-directional, because micro-entrepreneurs, too, manipulate the imaginary with some (albeit limited) freedom of expression and action. As it always happens, ideal types must be intended as abstract conceptualisations to deepen the understanding of a phenomenon, not as stereotypes: every real-life neo-craft entrepreneur will embody some hybrid combinations of these ideals.

The dramaturgical strategic user

The first ideal type is the dramaturgical strategic user. Belonging to this category are those who do not necessarily identify with the aesthetic regime of consumption and the set of values of the neo-craft imaginary, but are using them anyway, because they provide excellent opportunities to expand their business and express their craftsmanship. Thus, they are dramaturgical because they stage their participation to an economic imaginary despite remaining detached from it, and they are strategic in the use of the imaginary. Even though the attitude could be labelled as 'cynical', the detachment is felt towards the specific imaginary, not towards the work, practices and goods produced. In other words, detached strategic users are not less proud of their skills and goods produced, nor are they less passionate about their work: neo-craft entrepreneurs leaning towards this ideal type have sometimes controversially commented that, when you take out all the cool and fancy words, more enthusiastic adherents to the imaginary were not able to prepare and cook the meals properly and remained amateurs.

Neo-craft detached and strategic users typically had an already established entrepreneurial background or a professional past in the food or beverage industry. They use the imaginary as an add-on: they usually rely on other elements for the achievement of internal goods (e.g., economic success, and pride in their skills) and they employ the imaginary mainly for external goods (e.g., revenues and social prestige). As one micro-entrepreneur with a history in food retailing bluntly told me with an audacious metaphor, for him, adopting the gourmet food truck trend was akin to going from being a prostitute to being an escort. 'What is the difference?', he rhetorically asked me, before answering himself, 'If you call yourself an escort, you earn double'.

The compliant enthusiast

The second ideal type is the compliant enthusiast. They are the ones more passionately adhering to the aesthetic regime and the set of values of the imaginary, seeking to promote authentic modes of consumption as their mission. They are fully compliant with the imaginary, presenting a strong alignment between personal ethos and the values of the imaginary. Their will is to promote a certain food and beverage culture or to revive authentic forms of sociality: promoting locally produced food, cocktails based on a distinctive logic, and bars in which it is possible to recreate a kind of socialisation associated with old towns (see next the chapter of this volume). In short – and in line with the general meaning of authenticity – all that is not produced following a standardised, industrial logic. Neo-craft entrepreneurs leaning towards this ideal type are often the ones with a passion for crafts, food or drinks developed as a hobby, coming from white-collar jobs or directly from university.

The rebel activist

The third ideal type, which may be defined as the rebel activist, combines elements of the first and the second ideal types. The rebel activists are making use of the imaginary to pursue a cultural, social or political agenda. In their view, the promotion of values associated with the neo-craft economic imaginary is more important than the actual craft production of food and drinks. The economic imaginary is embraced to be then strategically and selectively used in the dimension more tightly linked with ethical and critical consumption. Sometimes the priority is explicit, as in the case of some groups opening a community bar or a restaurant because they felt it was the most coherent way to obtain economic independence while keeping up their own work on activism. Other times, the context is more nuanced, as in the case of a food truck owner promoting *quinto quarto* (literally 'the fifth quarter') food culture – that is, using only offal as ingredients, to promote alternative consumer cultures.

The passionate work of neo-craft entrepreneurs

> Listen, my boy, this work can be done only in two ways: the first is with the fixation on the trade unions, the fear of getting hurt and the desire to always stay at home, and the second one is with passion! Do you understand? The passion for this work. Even dead, but with passion! (Boris, season 2, episode 1)

This dialogue comes from the Italian cult television series Boris (2007–10), a satirical portrait of working life in a television studio. This is the moment in which the shady, unscrupulous unit production manager Sergio describes to the intern Alessandro, who had just suffered a workplace injury, how artistic and cultural work functions. Indeed, one of the many consequences of post-Fordist co-optation of authenticity was today's popular assumption that it is essential to combine personal passion and working identity. Inspirational quotes [...] like 'do what you love and you will never work a day in your life' are shared on enormous amounts of digital and physical images, with similar quotes attributed to Mark Twain or Confucius (albeit being probably coined by a Princeton philosophy professor in 1982), while in recent years life coaches have published myriad books on how to transform your job into your passion, your passion into your job, et cetera. Still, the trivialisation of passion and its wide use by managers as an enchantment technique (Endrissat et al., 2015) in order to better control and exploit employees does not imply that the idea of passion as a means to reach meaning in one's line of work should be disregarded as a fraud.

According to the accounts of the interviewed neo-craft entrepreneurs, the source of enjoyment and passion that they experience corresponds to the most fundamental concepts related to the imaginary: creativity (applying creativity and fantasy), authenticity (true human relations) and self-employment (confidence in themselves). These dimensions also play a role in preventing the alienating experiences hiding underneath the blanket concept of 'passion': neo-craft entrepreneurs expressed on multiple occasions how unprepared they were when they entered the neo-craft industries to face such levels of bureaucratic burden, physical fatigue and overwork. As one food truck owner I interviewed said: 'Days off are hard to get, zero leisure time, and private life is almost non existent. You may ask, why on earth am I doing this? It's my passion' (Ottaviano, food truck owner).

The passion for the job becomes the currency that makes it bearable to sacrifice external goods (e.g., the better social prestige offered by other professions, or higher profits) for internal goods. Still, enjoying internal goods and gaining social prestige through passionate work are two factors that often mix, as in the case of this food truck owner:

> Anyway, I haven't looked at this [business] mainly as a way of earning, but rather as my tool to spread an idea. So I can develop it thanks to the fact that one of the most important gastronomic critics in Italy called me and asked me to write a book, this for me is satisfaction. (Lamberto, food truck owner)

Two different books capture very well the two sides of the tension experienced by neo-craft entrepreneurs in their passionate work: *Willing*

Slaves of Capital by Frédéric Lordon (2014), and *The Amateur* by Andy Merrifield (2017). In *The Amateur*, Merrifield celebrates the creative and political potential of amateurism; that is, of doing what you love for the pleasure of it. The passionately engaged amateur stands in contrast to the bureaucratic professional as a model of an unalienated way of being. Amateurism emerges as powerful politics, a way to be passionate and effective activists. Amateurs find the sources of their pleasure in their 'hobby-horses', their passions to which they dedicate themselves, which can span from being as trivial as baking cakes at home or as majestic as making a revolution (among the illustrious cases of amateurs, Merrifield includes Marx, Lenin, Rosa Luxemburg). Neo-craft entrepreneurs resemble closely the amateurs described by Merrifield, but they also fundamentally differ in one aspect: they transform their hobby-horse into their job as well. This professionalisation, in the eyes of Merrifield, ruins everything: it 'transforms a labour of love into a loathing of labour' and 'annihilates the labour of love, that dowses the Hobby-Horsical flames of pure pleasure' (p. 159). In Merrifield, there seems to be an unresolved enigma regarding this fact. A job for him equates with professionalism, which as the flip side of amateurism is a source of all kinds of alienation. If any attempt to mix one's amateurish passion with the job ruins the benefits of the first, the only choices available for the individual seem the acceptance of an alienating life during work in exchange for an authentic life during leisure (as the classic, Fordist model promoted), or a privileged life of *otium* for people living off private income. Neo-craft entrepreneurs instead take a dangerous detour: they join the neoliberal narrative of becoming an entrepreneur and gaining the freedom of *doing what they love* without becoming 'professionals' (in Merrifield's meaning), continuing to approach their hobby-horse with the eyes of a passionate amateur. After all, some of the figures that Merrifield celebrates the most as examples of amateurs in his book display the same mixture between job and passions: the American journalist Jane Jacobs or the French philosopher Gilles Deleuze, who both became established professionals in their field but maintained an amateurish eye in front of their hobby-horses.

The tension between amateurish versus professional identity focuses mainly on the inner self of individuals. Lordon's (2014) analysis of capitalism in *Willing Slaves of Capital* focuses instead on the structural power held by late modern capitalism on the passions and desires of workers. Lordon combines the thought of Marx with the theories of Spinoza to argue that the real chains oppressing and alienating individuals are those of affection and desire, because social structures shape the desires and establish legitimate strategies to achieve them. The Marxian theory of economic relationships under capitalism is therefore reinterpreted through the idea of currency as a social relation and of money as the desire to which this relation gives birth (Lordon, 2014). The way capitalism keeps its dominion is by aligning wage labourers' desires to those of their employers, and of capitalism more generally, in a kind of 'joyful alienation'. Lordon's analysis – extremely useful to analyse the new context of neoliberalism – only examines waged labour, leaving contemporary widespread forms of self-employed work and micro-entrepreneurship out of the picture. Instead, this framework sheds light on critical aspects of neo-craft entrepreneurs' passionate work. The self-managed work of neo-craft entrepreneurs appears influenced by the structuring power of neo-liberal capitalism, while at the same time its autonomous nature allows greater freedom in misaligning their own trajectories of desire from the ones pre-determined by social structures. Neoliberalism uses their desires and passions to pursue the commodification of authenticity, creativity and the inner self, but they use the neoliberal model of entrepreneurship as a means to divert the meaning of these concepts towards different trajectories of desire; for example, prioritising non-monetary forms of reward.

Neo-craft entrepreneurs as meso-level dealers of taste

In the context of taste formation, circulation and consumption, neo-craft entrepreneurs carry out a specific and fundamental meso-level role. Their participation in the neo-craft industries depends critically on the symbolic values associated with such industries: craft work becomes a medium to achieve these intrinsic and extrinsic benefits. The symbolic work is not merely self-referential but has a deep multi-relational nature: it is linked to the aesthetic regimes of consumption, the economic imaginary, the related values, the materials and the customers. Entrepreneurs are cultural and symbolic intermediaries in all these processes between the macro level of taste formation and the micro level of everyday consumption processes, assembling authentic experiences for the customers. In other words, they are taste dealers (Gerosa, 2021), being the end actors of a neo-craft production chain, the ones who directly interact with consumers. The values composing the craft imaginary and the hip aesthetic regime, in general, can be analysed as floating signifiers, a term that Laclau (2006) formulated to describe the political claims gaining widespread relevance in society because they refer to loosely defined – but shared – meanings that can be embodied in highly individualised ways, giving birth to collective political mobilisations. Floating signifiers can be applied to consumers' mobilisations, too (Colleoni *et al.*, 2021). Authenticity itself is a good example of a floating signifier, as well as the fundamental values of the economic imaginary such as craft, typicality, tradition, etc., sharing an intrinsic ambiguity that allows their meaning to float.

De Certeau's (1984/2011) theory of strategies and tactics can help with the interpretation of the limited agency of taste dealing. In this context, strategies are the prerogative of actors able to operate at the macro level, with the goal of creating aesthetic regimes of consumption and economic imaginaries and preserving the hegemonic meaning of the floating signifiers supporting them. Tactics, instead, are the realm of taste dealers. A tactic, for de Certeau (p. 20) 'insinuates itself into the other's place, fragmentarily, without taking it over in its entirety, without being able to keep it at a distance. It has at its disposal no base where it can capitalize on its advantages, prepare its expansions, and secure independence with respect to circumstances.' Taste dealers insinuate themselves into an economic imaginary that other forces have built, introducing potentially divergent meanings to the floating signifiers composing it, but without the ability – if not in exceptional circumstances – to take over the hegemonic meanings. Being fragmented, small-scale and highly individualised due to their micro-entrepreneurial nature, such taste dealers can be very efficient at the local level but have little base over which to capitalise on their divergent framing and expand on larger scale sizes.

The practice of taste dealing by neo-craft entrepreneurs – as it emerged several times in this chapter – follows both the internal and external goods. Taste dealers' active role in translating the symbolic values of the imaginary to customers through the neo-craft goods in highly personalised ways reinforces the creative expression of the inner self, which is a fundamental dimension of authenticity. At the same time, this operation allows the accumulation of symbolic capital, through the display of one's proficiency in the taste dealing act, and the distinctiveness from other colleagues in what remains, after all, a highly competitive market. The neo-craft economic imaginary of consumption limits taste dealing by forcing it into a tight mesh of codified aesthetics and styles.

How the final neo-craft commodity served to the public is put together is another fundamental component of taste dealing, as it is proof of the manual and symbolic proficiency of the entrepreneurs and of their legitimate participation in the economic imaginary. The commodity becomes a real medium, whose highest goal is to transmit to customers not only a delicious consumption experience but also the emotions, values, and passion invested by the neo-craft entrepreneur in the process:

> Consumers return to me saying 'your cannolo is delicious' because they feel the emotions I convey through them . . . one time a girl bought a cannolo and afterwards came back to me crying . . . she was crying . . . I was really worried and I asked 'What happened?' and she answered 'I want to congratulate you because I am a pastry chef too, and when I ate your cannolo, beside the fantastic taste, I felt the emotion you infuse in it, and this makes the difference'. (Marco, food truck owner)

The taste dealing tactic needs to express the 'true self' of the neo-craft entrepreneur individually and distinctively from others, and it makes sense: the goal is to reinforce the symbolic reversal of any idea of standardisation which could recall industrial production and alienation. Authenticity, individuality and craft are therefore essential in the process of taste dealing:

> You must be authentic because otherwise you get considered the copy of someone else . . . or if you have a product that in reality is not from you, people realise it; I'm not saying everything must be artisanal, but at least the main product yes, it has to. (Tamara, food truck owner)

The value of typical ingredients and local productions is instrumental in accumulating symbolic capital as a skilful neo-craft taste dealer, and it reinforces the uniqueness of the offer to the customer. Neo-craft entrepreneurs spend a lot of time and effort to select exclusive, unusual providers for the raw ingredients used in their recipes, and they too must abide by the rules of the neo-craft economic imaginary. This operation requires a combination of personal taste and value choices, adherence to the rules of tradition, and rejection of commercial, mainstream market fads. The latter is a declaration of intents not always respected in the actual practices of neo-craft entrepreneurs, who must often reach a certain level of compromise to guarantee the economic viability of the enterprise. The following account from a micro-brewer and bar owner is a good example of this combination of factors:

> We often experiment, when selecting ingredients too. For example, we take Italian hops from a local producer in Reggio Emilia, we try the hops in small quantities, 20 or 30 litres, we see if we like the

> result and in case it's needed, we adjust what doesn't work. We are not a brewery that follows the fads, because we don't believe in them. We try to follow the styles. (Rino, bar owner)

The taste dealing process, however, concerns the entire consumption experience, not just the neo-craft product sold to the customer. As such, the entire shop environment and appearance, including the design of the place, the outlook and the performances of the neo-craft entrepreneur, the furniture, the music in the background, and the menu, contribute to sell the neo-craft economic imaginary – in the variant personalised by the single neo-craft entrepreneur – to the consumer. Neo-craft entrepreneurs devote extensive attention to the design of these aspects, knowing how relevant they are in building a proper promise of taste. The shop and the consumption experience as a whole become an extension and representation of the neo-craft entrepreneur's inner self and a further medium to transmit their values to consumers:

> Every 30 days we change the art installation hanging on the walls of the bar. That defines the creativity mark of the bar, in addition to the furniture. Our intention was precisely to put a strong accent in terms of creativity: whether it is photographers, clothing designers or painters, we are talking of creatives, thus we bring art into the bar . . . You always have to invent something in this kind of bar, it is not a posh bar in the city centre in which you go and you know everything is always identical; here people search for something different every time. (Norberto, bar owner)

Lights and shadows of neo-craft entrepreneurs taste dealing

Overall, the backbone of the neo-craft economy analysed in this chapter can be defined as a force for good: it sustains alternative production chains favouring other small producers, keeping local traditions alive; proposes alternative, more authentic and sustainable consumption practices; represents – in most cases – a more ethical alternative to mass-market industrial companies, known to cover their massive environmental and social negative externalities through cunning, deceitful 'greenwashing' marketing campaigns. The list could probably go on. However, it is also necessary to warn against a mythicisation of the neo-craft entrepreneurs' behaviour. As de Certeau's theory of strategies and tactics reminds us, they operate in the field of tactics, not of strategies. Inasmuch as a part of them can try to use the neo-craft economy to push a counter-hegemonic agenda, capitalism remains a decisive force in the development of the hip aesthetic regime of consumption and the neo-craft economic imaginary as well. In this sense, neo-craft entrepreneurs contribute to the commodification of authenticity. Furthermore, if the element of class is brought into the picture, neo-craft entrepreneurs ultimately appear as middle-class actors dealing authentic taste to middle-class consumers. This immediately reveals the exclusionary nature of the neo-craft industries: enjoying the fruit of taste dealing comes with a price; monetary and symbolic. To enjoy the authentic experience of consumption according to the neo-craft economic imaginary is the prerogative of those who can afford the price of gourmet street food, signature cocktails and handmade accessories, decoding the cultural sophistication behind these products. No matter how strong the political conscience of the owners of an artisanal bakery, their sourdough loaf made with locally and ethically sourced ingredients and craft techniques will always sell at prices inaccessible for many citizens.

The strong middle-class connotation of the neo-craft industries raises an issue of cultural and class appropriation. The food, beverages and, in general, many typical craft products that neo-craft entrepreneurs want to bring back to the wider public belong to working-class cultures of consumption. Street food such as *pizza a portafoglio* (a small pizza that can be folded, to be eaten standing) today is sold at significant prices to tourists and creative workers on their lunch break, but was once the only pizza that working-class people could afford. A Neapolitan worker from the past would have much preferred to sit down in a proper restaurant and eat a large *pizza Margherita* instead, to the dismay of contemporary omnivorous consumers (how dare they disregard Neapolitan typical street food for a standardised Margherita?!). If an Italian working-class individual who lived at the beginning of the twentieth century found themselves in a time warp and emerged in a contemporary hipster neighbourhood, they would remain extremely puzzled in front of all the bars disguised behind the names of old, humble professions or the highly sophisticated restaurants labelling themselves as inns or taverns. Taste dealers interpret the typical products, recipes and techniques to accommodate the palate of omnivorous customers, who wants to savour the symbolic imaginary of the pre-industrial genuine food but with the taste and quality of gourmet preparations.

Thus, taste dealing is also a process of invention of tradition (Hobsbawm and Ranger, 1992), which creates technicised myths (Jesi,

2014) of the past, functional in accommodating contemporary middle-class consumers, while simultaneously erasing working-class histories and traditions. This way, the only legitimate 'authentic' carbonara becomes the one prepared with *guanciale* (cheek lard) – even better if it comes from Amatrice, *pecorino romano* (sheep's milk cheese from Rome) and egg yolk. It doesn't matter that the original carbonara was probably – according to historians – an improvised food prepared out of necessity by coalmen during their long working trips, or a preparation by starving Roman citizens during the second world war with canned bacon and egg powder provided by American soldiers. This is not just a matter of historical mystification, but a mass upscaling of peasant food historically feeding the masses now translated into gourmet food exclusively reserved for the middle and upper classes. The implication is that neo-craft entrepreneurs as a collective force – despite their best intentions – could ultimately contribute to the erosion of the very same popular heritage that they wish to preserve. What is 'rediscovered' is only a limited amount of ingredients, products and techniques more easily translatable into the contemporary neo-craft economic imaginary through technicised myths, which then determine the new legitimate authentic versions of them. I wish the best of luck to anyone trying to serve an 'authentic carbonara' prepared with canned bacon and egg powder today in Italy: they'll soon find themselves running for their life. And for good reason: carbonara with guanciale, pecorino and yolk does actually taste delicious. The point is not to embark on a journey to discover the 'really authentic' pre-industrial food. Pre-industrial inhabitants of my territory, *Brianza*, up until the beginning of the twentieth century had a typical diet based on corn and rye bread, lard, milk and cornmeal mush, often mixed together. Personally, I'm very happy to stick to the gourmet carbonara instead. The point is to deconstruct the ideal of authenticity and become more detached from it, recognising that it is a social construct we embraced as a compass to reach a more meaningful life and make the world a better place. Authenticity should be adopted as a symbolic tool, not to reify an idealised version of the past but rather to inspire alternative, less alienating and commodified consuming paradigms for the future.

5
The hipster economy and the urban space

How could I describe the Milanese neighbourhood of NoLo[1] – where I conducted most of my ethnographic research – to a stranger? Well, I could start by saying it is a historically multicultural neighbourhood, just outside the city centre, which in recent times has sustained a flow of middle-class, creative and cultural workers choosing it for its affordable rents. I could go on by saying that walking through it you sense a vibrant atmosphere, thanks to street art murals and several independent art galleries, artisanal cafés, vintage clothing shops, each with its own unique offerings. I could add that by the evening it fills up with people visiting its trendy traditional restaurants, craft beer pubs and cocktail bars. Or, I could just say that it is a classic hipster neighbourhood, which would probably summarise all of the above.

When at the end of the second year of my PhD, after months of ethnographic research in NoLo, I was lucky enough to visit a number of European cities to attend academic conferences, I started a personal game that I named 'spot the local NoLo': walking through the city as a tourist, I looked for that one neighbourhood reflecting the same aesthetic and atmosphere as NoLo. It was very easy, to be fair: *Lavapiés* in Madrid, *Vesterbro* in Copenhagen, *Gloucester Road* in Bristol, to mention just the first cities that I visited. Obviously, they were the 'local NoLo' as much as NoLo was their Milanese counterpart. Every Western city worthy of its name nowadays has (more than) one 'hipster neighbourhood'. They are the trendiest places to live, the coolest epicentres of nightlife – and the most looked-after investment areas for real-estate companies. They are the neighbourhoods where the hipster economy is more densely concentrated, and thus becomes more apparent, defining the area's identity. Still, the hipster economy extends way beyond single neighbourhoods: it just materialises with different degrees of intensity and visibility. It also appears in hybrid configurations depending on contextual socio-economic factors. For example, when I relocated to Birmingham (United Kongdom) spending the first month in the 'migrant neighbourhood' of Sparkhill,[2] I was taken by surprise by the businesses of its so-called 'Balti-triangle'. They shared the same neo-craft economic imaginary of consumption typical of any hipster neighbourhood with some adaptation: almost everyone but me was of South Asian ethnicity, producing a different declination of the hip aesthetic displayed by shops, retailers and customers; not a single drop of alcohol was sold from the shops in the area, with cocktail bars and craft beer pubs being replaced by places specialising in 'mocktails' (non-alcoholic drinks), juices, milk-shakes and similar drinks.

The hip aesthetic regime of consumption and the neo-craft imaginary of consumption blend in not only at a territorial level but also by hybridising established business formulas, like the one of 'ethnic restaurants'. Once, entering a Chinese restaurant in Italy meant being able to order without even looking at the menu, regardless of the city you were in: the offering was highly standardised around a set of established dishes. Today, particularly in medium and large-sized cities, a shift can be observed from a standardised model to a hip, authentic aesthetic based on offering some unique flagship dishes and specialising in one regional cuisine or in a specific type of food (dumplings, soups, rice bowls, etc.). The hip aesthetic regime and the economic imaginary of consumption maintain a common codification, but they undergo a process of local vernacularisation. The same process of vernacularisation applies to the identity of the neighbourhoods: a codified aesthetic and economic imaginary descends on the urban fabric like a veil, covering everything with its texture, but adapting nonetheless to the specific shape of the area.

Overall, at the urban level, the hipster economy can be considered a 'force for good': it requalifies areas, sets the standards for a pleasurable and 'authentic' urban life, and provides an alternative – arguably more ethical – retail paradigm to multinational chain stores greedily devouring the urban space. However, today the hipster economy has become almost a synonym for some of the most severe threats to neighbourhoods, such as inequality, cultural homogenisation and gentrification. The present chapter will explore this tension, focusing on how neo-craft entrepreneurs contribute to shaping the development of hipster neighbourhoods following the same dynamic of accumulation and reproduction of symbolic capital analysed in the former chapter.

Sociability as a mission

> As I walk into the café, the owner welcomes me opening her arms and exclaiming: 'Come here, auntie's boy!'. She wears a colourful dress. I remain a bit hesitant. She may have noticed it as she takes a generous slice of cake and approaches, saying to me: 'This way, you will immediately catch the essence of this place: because I am the auntie and all of you are my nephews.' . . . When I am about to go, she greets me adding 'Now the beautiful thing would be if you would come to live in this neighbourhood! Auntie would organise you everything: I would find you a house, a good girl to get engaged to, everything!'
>
> (Ethnographic notes in NoLo)

These ethnographic notes were taken the second time I entered one café in the Milanese neighbourhood of NoLo to interview its owner. Despite the first time having been just a quick visit, she welcomed me with such intense warmth and enthusiasm that it initially left me disoriented. I later discovered that she was just the purest, ideal-typical embodiment of a mission embraced by most of the neo-craft entrepreneurs I interviewed: 'never lose the common aim, that is being together in these places', to quote a phrase she used. 'Being together' was elevated to a mission to be pursued as a collective action, with all the other shops: the aim was the creation of 'sociality for the pleasure of sociality', as the sociability (*Geselligkeit*) conceptualised by Georg Simmel (Simmel and Hughes, 1949). There is – again – a partially inescapable contradiction in it: the idealistic pursuit of sociality for the sake of it contrasts with the market goals of a shop. Still, many perceive the fostering of sociality in the neighbourhood as a 'social mission' equally valuable as its economic activity (and as other symbolic purposes related to food cultures, sociopolitical goals, etc.). Several neo-craft entrepreneurs that I interviewed mostly employed three connected strategies to promote sociability: the dealing of authentic social relations in the shop (often in parallel with the dealing of authentic taste seen in the previous chapter); the creation of an authentic atmosphere; the development of the shop as a territorial hub.

The dealing of authentic relations is often implemented by 'making customers feel like they are at home'. The idea of authentic self-expression translates into the intention to make customers feel as if they had entered the owners' personal space and met their most authentic side: 'I made available what in my opinion is the most precious thing that I have: myself. My humanity, my real self. I want to be authentic, sincere, and joyful with people. And this human component made the difference in my opinion' (Cinzia, bar owner).

The dealing of sociability goes hand in hand with the creation of an authentic space enabling social interactions. The design of the shop becomes an integral part of the display of the unique inner self of the entrepreneur and of putting together a welcoming, home-like environment. This can mean introducing very mundane elements, like in the case of Cinzia who transformed her passion for collecting rubber ducks into the cornerstone around which she built the distinctive identity of the café and more authentic relationships with customers. Her café became a 'house of duckies', on an explicitly playful register. The positioning of the owner's personal collection of rubber ducks contributes to the authentic atmosphere permeating the bar: each duck has its name, thus its own identity and specificity, amplifying the aura of the authentic atmosphere. Moreover, the authenticity aura becomes interactive by its own nature because customers are invited to contribute to it by bringing their own rubber ducks (even from trips abroad: exotic rubber ducks!) to be displayed at the shop. This makes them active participants in assembling the aura, reinforcing the friendship between customers and the owner – which also translates into customer retention.

This phenomenon makes neo-craft entrepreneurs stand out because of the social function they perform in the neighbourhood. They frame themselves as members of the community – contributing to its everyday social life, needs and aspirations – and not just as commercial actors. They organise events devised to be moments of connection with the neighbourhood's social life. In these moments, neo-craft entrepreneurs do something good for the community, reinforce the social ties with and between the local inhabitants, and pay back the community for what they have received, economically and humanely. These community-building practices are also a movement 'back to the future', tightly linked with the temporal dimension of the neo-craft economic imaginary of consumption: symbolically, neo-craft entrepreneurs wish to recreate social relations associated with an idealised pre-industrial urban environment, which supposedly got lost in the present time. However, these values are projected in the contemporary (neoliberal) city, and clearly interact with the tenets of the *sharing economy* ideology now powerfully shaping urban economies and development policies (Salice and Pais, 2017). Sociability becomes the pillar around which to recreate an authentic urban community, modelled on a fictional myth of the past, to overcome the alienation of contemporary urban life, allegedly characterised by atomisation and fake relationships. This project, despite some evident nostalgic – sometimes even reactionary – elements, also recovers old core aspects of the revolutionary politics of authenticity of the 1960s and 1970s: one slogan of the French May 1968 uprising was 'talk to your neighbours!'. An example of the relevance of such a project is the remarkable initiative of one café owner that I interviewed, who started to organise (free) lunches with customers at his personal home on Sundays. Initially prompted by personal loneliness, the event later acquired stronger social traits:

> It is a matter of reciprocating the affection of my customers, that even cease to be customers and become friends, a part of the family. Because here we are creating a large family, do you understand? The people that come here for lunch become part of the family. We are creating this because everything related to socialising with people has been lost over time. Socialisation, being together and among people, even the typical Sunday lunch with relatives, all of it has vanished, is not a tradition anymore. (Carlo, bar owner)

As the dealing of sociability persists over time, some neo-craft shops become social hubs in the neighbourhood. Other neo-craft entrepreneurs design their shops as such from the beginning, like in this example:

> This café is dedicated to families and kids, the reason for opening it was satisfying some necessities of the neighbourhood, and also personal... We opened this place to work on the community of families and kids of the neighbourhood, focusing on toys, children's books, and this kind of elements. In the beginning, this was the idea. Then it evolved according to the necessities of the entire neighbourhood and its inhabitants, also of the ones that do not have kids: the need to have a coffee place that could foster community-building and become a meeting place. (Mara, café owner)

When such a transformation happens, the achievement of internal and external goods blends in the pursuit of sociability. The lunches organised by Carlo resemble meals among friends, external to the realm of economic transactions. When customers wish to contribute, he invites them to bring a good bottle of wine or a dessert (the only course he does not prepare), in a way that – going back to the comparison with the sharing economy – resembles the interactions of reciprocity rather than of market exchange. From the quote above, Mara may sound like a community organiser more than an entrepreneur. Still, the pursuit of the internal good of sociability, directly or indirectly, also reflects on the economic revenues of the shop and the prestige of the entrepreneurs in the community. As Mara herself recognises, talking about a renowned social enterprise award she won: 'Leading a business that also has social value is important both to stand out to the public and to make work more pleasurable for the people employed by such business'. In the everyday economic life of a business, the pursuit of economic profit is a necessary pre-condition. As such, sociability becomes – like food cultures analysed in the previous chapter – a technicised myth, bent to economic profit in contradiction with its own nature.

The logic of the village

The accounts from neo-craft entrepreneurs are a testimony of their agency in shaping the contemporary urban space and what, visually, has come to be defined as 'hipster neighbourhoods', particularly where their spatial concentration gets stronger. Similarly to their behaviour in the field of consumption, neo-craft entrepreneurs in the urban sphere recover a logic of the pre-industrial urban village as a means to build a future authentic urban life characterised by sociability, against the atomisation and hollowness of present urban relationships. Still, as repeatedly observed in the previous chapters, the hipster economy is a meso-level phenomenon, and by implication this means that neo-craft entrepreneurs have a limited, bounded agency. They intercept, adopt and manipulate aesthetic dispositions and economic imaginaries that they can influence, but they do not primarily create or shape them. Aesthetic dispositions and economic imaginaries are the complex outcome of historical processes where macro-level actors have a predominant role. As such, the hipster economy in urban spaces constitutes a converging spot between these pushes: a product of individual aspirations of living in authentic urban spaces, it is nonetheless functional to corporate financial exploitation. The logic of the village in the contemporary urban scenario is the outcome of top-down creative discourses promoted by wide coalitions of macro-actors and bottom-up processes – and this process started long ago.

In 1992, the then Prince of Wales launched the UK 'urban villages forum', to promote the birth of new urban villages. What was an urban village, according to the forum? The definition given was of a new settlement of around 3,000–5,000 people, realised on greenfield or brownfield, 'small enough to create a community in the truest sense of the word – a group of people who support each other, but big enough to maintain a reasonable cross-section of facilities. Walking determines the size – a 10-minute walk from one side to the other' (Huxford, 1998). Its nostalgic, 'neo-traditionalist' nature was explicit: the objective was to recreate an urban fabric composed of multiple small villages – modelled after the early industrial ones – to counter the alienation of contemporary suburbs. As the Prince of Wales rhetorically asked when launching the project: 'Why, given that traditional urban environments worked so well in the past, do we seem incapable of building places with these same qualities today?' (Neal, 2003, p. 5). The urban village model was inspired by the American critique to architectural modernism and rationalism made famous by Jane Jacobs in the *Death and Life of Great American Cities* and by the paradigm of 'new urbanism', based on the two pillars of community-building and sustainability.

The urban village forum initiative never really caught on apart from a few cases, but the Prince of Wales can probably claim moral victory. The logic of the urban village has become a major force. Planning models envisioning a polycentric city, a 'city of quarters' (Jayne and Bell, 2017) largely took over models distinguishing between a city centre and the development of suburbs. New innovative urban models such as the 'sharing city', the 'smart city' and the 'new municipalism' – ideally putting sharing economy principles and technological progress at the service of citizens – put community building and sustainability at the core of their agenda. The idea of a 15-minute city – where all inhabitants can reach every service they need within 15 minutes, either by foot, bike or public service – has been recently proposed by multiple actors and is getting adopted by a growing number of municipal administrations, including Paris and Milan. These planning models combine the nostalgic appeal to old-time urban landscapes with the use of highly modern solutions and discourses, focusing on inhabitants' wellbeing.

I do not claim that the urban village forum has the merits for this escalation. Clearly, the essential element for this success was the spread of discourses on creative cities, industries and class, which became a paradigmatic urban development model from the new millennium onwards (Gerosa, 2022), especially through the famous and controversial *The Rise of the Creative Class* by Richard Florida (2002). Applying the tenets of human capital growth theory to creativity and the contemporary city, it tied urban development to the ability of neighbourhoods to attract the new creative middle class (the reference category of the hipster economy). The urban village forum idea is just a testimony to the fact that the same push to refocus urban planners' attention towards the neighbourhood, and remodel it after an ideal old village, was already present, and it came from long-standing calls for recreating authentic urban spaces.

The prompt by Florida to classify cities in a performance list of attractiveness for creative workers started a global competition between cities – and even neighbourhoods – for place branding. Contemporary cities increasingly look like a series of neighbourhoods patched together, each striving to brand itself with a distinctive identity. The presence of the basic requirements to boot up such a place branding process seems to be the new discriminating factor in urban development between thriving and 'dormitory' neighbourhoods. Obviously, despite the new ambitious planning models, poorer suburbs remain largely excluded by this new horizon of possibilities. Since one essential ingredient in this race seems to be the presence of a hip lifestyle, the promotion of the hip urban village logic has become a priority for local and national political actors, willing to improve the urban branding of their city *vis-à-vis* its competitors. Furthermore, large coalitions of investors, bankers and corporate actors have further backed these processes, in search of ways to further fuel the hypertrophic contemporary financial economy through real-estate investments. In most cases this happens through symbolic framing, but sometimes it happens literally, as well: the neighbourhood in which I currently live in Birmingham claims at its entrance to be a 'village', as a few others also do. Despite these claims having some historical foundation – the neighbourhoods were once villages before being incorporated into the city of Birmingham – the areas claiming this unofficial status for themselves tend to be the ones with a greater fame of hip neighbourhoods. As a Reddit user commented when I asked more information on this village labelling, 'If you live somewhere calling itself a village, sorry, but the price of beer is about to massively increase'.

Indeed, the hipster economy integrates the logic of the urban village in the consumption sphere. The network of small and independent shops embedded in the local community resemble an idealised version of the retailing landscape of old villages. The hipster economy's goal of guaranteeing the experience of authenticity to its members – neo-craft entrepreneurs or consumers – parallels the broader urban village goal of providing an authentic urban life to its inhabitants. After all, the logic of the urban village shares with the hipster economy its goal of offering an alleged 'alternative to the mainstream' (i.e., the old industrial, modernist urban paradigm predominant during the Fordist age), while being itself a new paradigm based on notions of authenticity and distinctiveness from every other urban place. Both are products of the same quest for authenticity in opposition to the alienation of the Fordist industrial society, contrasting it in the consumption sphere or in urban design. Both paradigms are also at the same time well embedded phenomena in the neoliberal society, envisioning possible paths to overcome its failures. Finally, both share an intrinsic ambiguity, characterising them from their origins.

Indeed, Jane Jacobs' thought – which can be considered the intellectual foundation of the logic of the village – already display some tensions, when analysed in its entirety. In books such as *The Economy of Cities* and *Cities and the Wealth of Nations*, she was instrumental in introducing the idea of cities as the most fundamental source of economic growth, foregrounding discourses on endogenous growth theory, the creative city and Florida's subsequent theory of creative capital. Florida and Robert Lucas, for their part, cited Jacobs's thought as a pivotal influence for their works. The logic of the urban village produced both the conditions for more authentic urban experiences and for the neoliberal exploitation of the urban fabric through extreme strategies of place branding and inter-neighbourhood competition. Like for the hip aesthetic regime of consumption and the neo-craft economic imaginary of consumption, the logic of the urban village became a symbolic battleground for hegemony between corporate goals of capital accumulation and exploitation and the ideally liberating projects of industrious micro-entrepreneurs and consumers.

An urban village for whom?

As previously analysed, two of the most serious negative externalities generated by authenticity as an aesthetic regime of consumption are a new codification of styles and aesthetics – which replace the previous standardisation of consumption objects – and the upscaling and cultural appropriation of popular consumption cultures. The logic of the village, as further proof of its tight relationship with the hipster economy, has come to be associated with the same issues, under the form of cultural homogenisation and gentrification.

Sharon Zukin, especially in *Loft Living* (1982) and *Naked Cities* (2010), provided exemplary analyses of the development and intricacy of these phenomena. Zukin's general premises and goals are in some way similar – on a greater scale and depth – to the ones of this book. Her fundamental assumption is that in emerging post-industrial capitalism, capital accumulation depends increasingly on cultural consumption and the mantra of authenticity. Thus, her analysis focuses on the interaction between the lifestyle of individuals and the macro-processes of capital accumulation in the new urban configuration, dominated by the once rebellious and now commodified polar star of authenticity. In *Naked Cities*, Zukin pointedly denounces the paradoxical outcomes of gentrification and homogenisation that derive from the apparently laudable goal to build authentic urban places, but the contradictions inherent to the urban hipster economy and the logic of the village are already illustrated in *Loft Living*, published 28 years before:

> First, the changes in the use of space that promise to reconstitute an urban middle class really effect the reconquest of the city's core for upper-class users. Second, the historic preservation that local businesses accept in order to compete with shopping centers and national chains turns all downtowns into versions of Faneuil Hall. Third, the revitalization projects that claim distinctiveness – because of specific historic or aesthetic traits – become a parody of the unique. (Zukin, 1982, p. 190)

The almost 30 years between *Loft Living* and *Naked Cities* are further proof of the long historical development of a hip aesthetic regime of consumption that maintained common elements from its origins to its stage of maturity. Indeed, these phenomena anticipated the current reality of urban cities. From the Greenwich Village in New York – which could be considered the symbolic forefather of all urban villages – to today's latest hipster neighbourhoods, an apparently unbreakable cycle of gentrification processes happened in which real-estate investors exploit the new cool aura of specific areas to bleed them dry from the inside, building luxury residential housing to feed financial capitalism and thereby expelling migrant and working-class inhabitants, first, and then the same creative middle class who triggered the process. The construction of luxury apartments largely fails to answer social demand, but responds to a financial logic, with real estate becoming an asset. This process has a domino effect: the hip middle class relocates in other neighbourhoods with similar features, subsequently triggering the same process there (in New York City, after Greenwich Village came Soho, Dumbo, NoLiTa, Williamsburg, etc.).

The gentrification of urban places is connected to their cultural homogeneity. A group of Italian researchers (Barbera *et al.*, 2022) recently published an edited book provocatively called *Against Villages* ('*Contro i Borghi*' in Italian). The subtitle, 'The nation forgetting its towns', clarifies the nature of the critique advanced by the authors: from the 1990s onwards, the village has become the scenario for an idyllic imaginary of development built around ecological, economic and cultural sustainability, promising authenticity but bringing touristification and foodification. These processes reduce the rural 'village' to a glossy façade where one goes for a few days on holiday or stops by to enjoy typical, authentic experiences of consumption, but where the real distinctive history and specificity of the place are erased and the original local community is ignored.

The 'village' that the Italian researchers discuss is the small rural town, but the same argument remains valid for urban villages as well. As Zukin observes, the valorisation of historical buildings and the place branding based on the uniqueness of the neighbourhood becomes a parody, because all hip neighbourhoods end up looking similar. As the opening of the present chapter stressed, hip neighbourhoods adopting the logic of the village reach a common paradoxical status of 'conformist distinctiveness': they are all distinctive, but in the same way. This applies at a truly global level, given the current influence of the hip aesthetic regime of consumption and of contemporary planning models. Netflix's documentary series *Midnight Asia*, which aired in 2022, presents the nightlife of six Asian metropolises (Tokyo, Seoul, Mumbai, Bangkok, Taipei and Manila). I watched it with the feverish attention that only a researcher can have when discovering the very phenomena they are studying in different contexts. I ended up feeling amazed and frightened at the same time, thinking: 'the hipster economy really is an Asian phenomenon, too, then!' The homogeneity in the narration of the nightlife of the six cities was astonishing: each city had the cocktail bar with eclectic mixologists creating their own signature cocktails with local ingredients, blending different traditions; the street-food vendor – managed by traditional owners with innovations brought by younger generations – rediscovering the typical ingredients and recipes of the local food culture with a unique twist, maintaining its popular spirit while serving thousands of inhabitants and tourists; a local music scene allowing new generations to express their true self outside the boundaries of the alienating society. Even accounting for the likely choice of showing just what they thought a mainly Western audience would find cool to watch, the hipster economies of the six Asian megalopolises not only closely resembled each other, but they also resembled every other hip neighbourhood in the global West.

All these considerations led me to ponder for which inhabitants the authentic urban village is really designed, and which is the community to which it refers and whose interests does it serve. Sharon Zukin in *Loft Living* acknowledges that the contradictions of the logic of the urban village can be described as the fact that 'the realization of ideas in urban space re-creates an unequal distribution of the benefits that these ideas represent' (Zukin, 1982, p. 190). It is not that the ideas are wrong, the issue is how they are applied. These processes mostly happen above the heads of local retailers and inhabitants and beyond their intention: their main responsibility can be considered not to realise until it is too late – or to refuse to acknowledge – how their deserving symbolic work in reality feeds a capitalist machine that serves only the God of money, dismissing other principles. They naively think that their specific case will be different from all the others, or fatalistically consider that it is not even worth trying steer the process, given the disparity of forces between them and the macro-actors at play. But there is something that individuals in their role of consumer and of cultural and taste intermediaries can achieve. In *Naked Cities*, Sharon Zukin extensively delves into the topic arguing that, although authenticity can be held largely responsible for the homogenisation and gentrification of contemporary cities, it also contains the revolutionary potential to liberate cities from these forces:

> Authenticity is nearly always used as a lever of cultural power for a group to claim space and take it away from others without direct confrontation, with the help of the state and elected officials and the persuasion of the media and consumer culture. We can turn this lever in the direction of democracy, however, by creating new forms of public-private stewardship that give residents, workers, and small business owners, as well as buildings and districts, a right to put down roots and remain in place. (Zukin, 2010, p. 246)

Similarly, the authors of *Against Villages* propose a politics for towns – stripped of the 'village' branding label – which looks at the interests and the quality of everyday life of every member of the community, especially the long-standing inhabitants and the most vulnerable. This would mean rejecting those notions of community that exclusively consider the new members of the new hip middle class, thereby producing forms of selective empowerment in the urban village (Gerosa and Tatari, 2021), to overcome abstract proclamations of involvement of all categories of inhabitants, and it would also mean directly recognising and solving matters of inequality. It would need bold shifts in behaviour by neo-craft entrepreneurs and new inhabitants, renouncing to the immediate spillover that the marketing-oriented authenticity branding guarantees, in order to embrace a more critical, ethical and political consciousness. It would mean engaging a battle to reconquer the hegemonic meaning and use of authenticity from the capitalist forces, which appropriated it from countercultures more than 50 years ago. A daunting task, indeed, but the only one that, paraphrasing Zukin's conclusions, could mark a new beginning and restore an authentic urban life.

Concluding remarks: the past, present and future of the hipster economy

Le hipster est mort, vive le hipster economy!

While discussing with colleagues the title of the present book during the long months of its gestation, a couple of considerations – often combined – were prevalent. On the one hand, a pleasing acknowledgement regarding its potential catchiness. On the other, a question of concern: 'Haven't hipsters already gone out of fashion?' The answer cannot but be affirmative: any reader only quickly glancing at the title of this book could conclude its obsolescence occurred way before reaching the bookshelves. However, for the patient reader leafing through the chapters, it will become clear that by placing the hipster economy in the spotlight, this book has contemporarily celebrated the death – or the irrelevance – of the hipster as a stereotypical subcultural figure and the rise of hipsterism as a widespread, paradigmatic aesthetic of consumption. Hipsters are – or have been – one of the most visible expressions of this tendency thanks to their manifest ostentation of these features, the persistence of their faith, and the conundrum of highly debatable contradictions generated by the pursuit of 'pure authenticity' in consumption. As such, they were condemned to be a fad, like many other subcultures impersonating the accrual of certain symbolic values in their purest form. Differently from these other subcultures, however, which usually represented the medley of marked countercultural elements with mainstream desires of alternativeness, the hipster walked through the coolest neighbourhoods of Western societies as the herald of the newly established mainstream paradigm, embodying purely its ethos and values. While the heralds inevitably fell into irrelevance as quickly as they rose to prominence, their hipsterist aesthetic disposition reinforced itself as a low-key diffused and persistent gravitational force.

In *The Royal Touch*, Marc Bloch famously argued that there is no greater sign of victory for a long-disputed belief, than to be demoted to the rank of banality. In the same years, Gramsci conceptualised cultural hegemony as a condition met when some cultural perspectives become widely accepted in society as a pure matter of fact. This book has hopefully provided ample evidence of how the taste for the authentic, often mediated by a neo-craft economic imaginary, has become a taken-for-granted driving force to be reckoned with in late modern capitalism. This is how the provocation in the introduction of this book – that contrary to the widespread mocking of hipsters, middle-class individuals are all someway hipsterist as consumers – has been proven faithful. This explains why the hipster label has become such a fitting description of the contemporary urban economy but is mostly useless to distinguish individual consumer choices – if not for friendly banter or ironic mocking: is ordering an IPA more hipster than disdainfully rejecting it to demonstrate appreciation for a cask ale beer? Is going to a highly distinctive cocktail bar – where a mixologist prepares an original selection of their current creations – more hipster than choosing an old bar that has been opened for decades where an old owner coarsely serves traditional cocktails? Is dining at a place serving gourmet street food prepared only with local ingredients from small producers more hipster than sneaking into an ethnic restaurant where all other clients are 'locals', menus are written in a foreign language and portions are as abundant as they are greasy? Sometimes, one could end with the impression that hipsterism as an aesthetic disposition has occupied the entire spectrum of possibilities for urban consumption, becoming an inescapable fate. Despite such an impression being an overt exaggeration, its daunting perception is indicative.

The hipster economy as a lens to analyse capitalism's history

This book has developed an ambitious theoretical framework composed by a *longue durée* reading of society, macro-level aesthetic regimes of consumption and meso-level economic imaginaries of consumption, with the goal of giving back to the analysis of consumption processes and tastes the place that it deserves, but that has mostly been negated, in the studies of the history of capitalism. Through this model, it employed the hipster economy as an empirical lens to advance three fundamental arguments in relation to modern capitalism, which can be differentiated according to the grade of historical depth that is adopted. Keeping the focus on the past couple of decades – what we could refer to as late neoliberalism – the hipster economy hints at the rise of a powerful neo-craft economic imaginary that has elevated the craft object of consumption as the standard to which both small artisans and large industrial producers strive for, thanks to its auratic display of authentic taste, and that is also redefining the envisioned standards of meaningful work. The neo-craft imaginary of consumption has clear parallels with the arts and crafts movement of the late eighteenth century, which, in light of subsequent history, has often been harshly interpreted as a tardive wake of an idealistic resistance to the process of industrialisation. The resurgence of neo-craft industries did justice to its memory, ultimately proving to be an astonishing act of defiance and resilience against what, for the most part of the twentieth century, has appeared to be the inexorable tendency of history to steer towards a more intense standardised industrial production, led by the undisputed predominance of Fordism over both sides of the Iron Curtain. From this viewpoint, it is really true what Sandra Alfoldy (2018, p. 82) argued by saying that 'if William Morris were alive today I do not doubt he would also run a micro-brewery, most likely fermenting yeast from his own beard' – and crying with joy, I would add. In further similarity with its predecessor, the neo-craft economic imaginary is deeply entrenched with ethical values and visions of fairer futures. With a critical difference: for Morris, craft production was a way to elevate the alienated manual labour of the mass of proletarian workers into meaningful labour (through the addition of artistic value), in a step towards the overthrowing of capitalism and the accomplishment of a socialist society; the neo-craft economy imaginary instead points at reintroducing a deeper relationship with the material and manual dimension in the life of the middle class alienated by industrial society, in order to achieve a more meaningful, authentic life experience.

On a deeper level of historical analysis, distancing our viewpoint from the past few decades to the past 50 years, the analysis of the hipster economy and of the related neo-craft economic imaginary of consumption enables us to recognise in the hip aesthetic regime of consumption a fundamental but largely overlooked feature of post-Fordism. This aesthetic regime of consumption originated in the need to find new ways to make the saturated consumer society of the sixties porous again to the injection of new commodities, letting the flow of capital circulate, and the concurrent necessity to address the multifaceted revolt experienced by most Western societies between the 1960s and 1970s against the standardisation, alienation and commodification of human life imposed by

Fordism (also in the field of consumption). The realisation of an alternative to these nefarious features has passed by the ultimate guiding value of authenticity as the conceptual opposite of alienation. The birth, development and maturity stage of the hip aesthetic regime of consumption all derive from the dialectical relationship between these two conceptual antagonists. In the 1970s, alienation became a buzzword on everyone's lips in public debates: in an overview for the *Annual Review of Sociology*, sociologist Melvin Seeman (1975, p. 91) defined it as a 'master concept – conveniently imprecise, empirically omnipresent, and morally irresistible when employed as a critique'. Fifty years later, in the phase of full maturity of the hip aesthetic regime of consumption (of which the hipster economy is a symbol), the same can be argued for authenticity: conveniently imprecise, empirically omnipresent and morally irresistible when employed as an aspirational standard.

The contextualisation of the neo-craft economic imaginary into the wider hip aesthetic regime of consumption allows for the recognition of the consumer-led nature of the hipster economy. Still, adopting an even deeper historical perspective encompassing not just the late phase of modern capitalism, but its entire history, the paradigmatic hip aesthetic regime of consumption can be likewise contextualised in the broader contested relationship between human nature and the modern, industrial society. The dialectics between alienation and authenticity in the past 50 years is but the last iteration of a process already recognisable in the accounts of Jean Jacques Rousseau, and possibly beyond. In other words, the contemporary valorisation of the individual as an autonomous subject and the harsh repression of its qualities has been an intrinsic feature, almost a trademark, of the entire modern industrial capitalist history. This does not suggest a positivist account of history, implying odd and obsolete notions about the end of history. However, it does suggest the usefulness of adopting a *longue durée* approach to get a comprehensive grasp of the contemporary meaning of authenticity (and conversely, of alienation), that the book has advanced.

Some theses on the future of the hipster economy

As we come to the end of our brief but dense examination of the hipster economy, it is impossible to resist the temptation to venture into the realm of future speculations – fitting the role of the diviner more than that of the social scientist – and to trace some paths of possible future development. In an effort to limit the high probability of running into gross errors, such speculations will limit themselves to highlighting the major tensions and junctures that can be foreseen in the future of the hipster economy and of the quest for authenticity. May reality have mercy on these paragraphs.

In accomplishing this task, it may be useful to continue observing the distinction between the immediate future and longer processes. In the short term, a pivotal aspect is the outcome of the perennial conflicting co-existence in the hipster economy between corporate and countercultural pushes, derived from the intrinsically ambiguous nature of authenticity in post-Fordist capitalism – possibly the biggest difference between late modern capitalism and precedent configurations – which can be understood as both an ideal for individual self-expression against alienation and at the same time a tool for the commodification of human life. 'Cannibal capitalism', to quote the recent vivid and fitting definition by Nancy Fraser (2022), avid for any societal phenomenon in the incessant need to sustain its quest for profit-making, devoured even the aspiring dream of freedom from capitalism itself, in a perverse ouroboros. Interpreted in such a way, the hipster economy is only the latest occurrence of what Mark Fisher describes as capitalist pre-corporation, 'the pre-emptive formatting and shaping of desires, aspirations and hopes by capitalist culture', which has made ideas such as 'alternative' and 'independent' to be 'styles, in fact *the* dominant styles, within the mainstream' (Fisher, 2012, p. 9). What is certain is that the commodification of authenticity by late modern capitalism is progressively consuming and exhausting its meaning and salience not just for commodifying purposes, but for any other use – including countercultural ones.

Here the flash in the pan of hipster subculture represents a daunting reminder for the hipster economy. From the 1970s to today, the consumption of authentic experiences has had to pass through several stages of cultural and symbolic refinement to remain appetible in the eyes of the customer. The appreciation for the authentic – as the tripartite definition of authenticity in this book demonstrated – implies, by definition, the disdain for the commercial, thus the commercialisation of the authentic takes the form of an unnatural operation, that quickly depletes any used object or phenomenon of consumption of its authentic aura. The realm of authentic phenomena and commodities to which it is possible to inscribe an authentic aura, however, is not infinite, and the first signs of this limitation are coming to the surface. In the field of digital marketing and advertising, for example, the pioneering use of endorsing celebrities because of their authenticity has been substituted with the use of social media influencers, celebrated for their more authentic relationship with consumers. With the presence of sponsored content promoted by influencers becoming omnipresent, to counter their loss of credibility, marketers turned their attention to micro-influencers, which rapidly became the new celebrated champions of authenticity: the illusion of the intimate connection that they are able to maintain with their small, highly targeted audiences provides an authentic aura incomparably superior to the worn-out one of macro-influencers. Still, the widespread commercialisation of micro-influencers is rapidly wearing out their authenticity just as well. Despite odd neologisms as 'genuinfluencers' or 'deinfluencers' exposing the attempts by micro-influencers to reinforce their authentic claims by refusing or dissimulating commercial goals, what could come next is yet to be seen. The same could be argued for most major fields of consumption of the urban hipster economy. An Instagram page celebrating the rediscovery of old-fashioned, traditional Milanese restaurants and taverns that have been left untouched by the passage of time, and mostly attracting younger audiences of middle-class hip consumers, has named itself 'sincere places' ('*posti sinceri*' in Italian), arguably to distinguish their experience from the contemporary cathedrals of authentic consumption analysed throughout this book. Similarly, it is possible that in the longer term, the symbolic depletion of the concept of authenticity and its re-proposition and declination *ad nauseam* to consumers in myriad different occurrences will bring capitalism to the necessity of identifying other, related floating signifiers with which to express the same aspirations.

At the same time, the long history of authenticity as a social and political ideal before its incorporation by late modern capitalism requires taking into serious consideration the survival of its political subversive potential, even if just – to follow the famous Gramscian quote – to counter the pessimism of the intellect with the optimism of the will. The fact that late modern capitalism has engaged with its preponderant resources in a symbolic struggle to domesticate and hold the hegemonic meaning of authenticity, does not mean that alternative uses of the concept have been crushed or forced into irrelevance. On the contrary, there are multiple signs that the 2020s of this new century represent the mature phase of re-politicisation of Western societies after the long ebb into the private sphere that started in the 1980s. The undeniable condition of polycrisis affecting the globe – recognised even by venues such as the World Economic Forum in Davos – is pushing an increasing number of spontaneous movements to recognise, more or less directly, neoliberal capitalism as the obstacle to be variously eradicated or reformed to avoid falling into dooming dystopias or more plainly into the extinction of (not only) human life. The cost-of-living crisis has fostered factually controversial but symbolically influential phenomena such as the so-called 'great resignation' and more in general a multiplicity of social movements calling for the right to fair housing and decent living standards. The looming environmental collapse led to the birth of influential transnational social movements such as Fridays for Future and Extinction Rebellion, and to myriad national similar organisations. Anti-racist and transfeminist social movements are gaining ground in the wake of widespread mobilisations such as #blacklivesmatter and #metoo. Furthermore, the Covid-19 pandemic turned out to be a formidable further accelerator of these tendencies.

Beyond the parallel with the 1970s, this new wave of societal politicisation also bears significant peculiarities; among them is the pivotal role played by consumption and lifestyles. The hip aesthetic regime of consumption provides the ideal platform to sustain these efforts, and a privileged ground for the re-politicisation of authenticity on more radical pathways. This way, the urban hipster economy could effectively do its part to achieve the goal shared by its most politically engaged fringes, of being part of a movement over and beyond neoliberalism. As the hip aesthetic regime of consumption can only be understood in combination with the relative regime of production and mode of regulation, in the same way, the subversive potential of the hipster economy can only be considered jointly with wider societal movements. The current frequent accusations towards the hipster economy of not being enough, not radical enough, not bringing a substantive change, not standing up to its ideals, equally to the specular acritical exaltation of its supposed salvific potential, all suffer from the same drawback: they have in some way incorporated an implicit neoliberal perspective that sees the individual, as the consumer or entrepreneurial self, as the protagonist of social change; they expect from the hipster economy alone what it cannot accomplish. This perspective has, obviously, often been adopted by members of the hipster economy itself. Only by dropping this presumption can the subversive potential of the hipster economy emerge. Alone, the hipster economy is doomed to remain the expression of and functional to a middle-class moral posture, incapable of having a transformational impact on the phenomena it criticises. As a component of wider social coalitions, it contains in itself – thanks to its ability to interpret and intercept the consuming desires of large components of society – the potential to contribute to the re-establishment of authenticity as a powerful agent of subversive social change.

Looking beyond the short-term battle over the hegemonic meaning of authenticity, at least a couple more future tendencies can be outlined, which currently remain in the stage of hypotheses. The first possible tendency, which could develop in the medium term, is a possible appropriation of the neo-craft economic imaginary and consequently of ideals of authenticity by the right-wing movements that represent the other half of the sky of the current highly polarised political spectrum of Western societies almost everywhere. Indeed, up until now in this book as well as in society, the neo-craft economic imaginary has been naturally associated with a middle class imbued with progressive values composing, from a political point of view, the backbone of Western social-democratic (and often leftist) parties. The gradual shift of Western social-democratic parties towards the implicit adherence to the progressive liberal values of 'woke capitalism' (Rhodes, 2021) is at the base of the current ambiguity displayed by the hipster economy and just extensively discussed. However, 'woke capitalism' represents only one bifurcation of current capitalism. The other bifurcation corresponds to what Sergio Bologna (2021) defines lucidly as 'neo-Nazism without Hitler'; that is, the encounter between the pervasive force of neoliberalism and the enduring nationalistic values, resulting in a peculiar fusion of individualism and neo-fascism. Despite notorious links between right-wing populism and the new working class, the neoliberal neo-fascist ethics is well diffused in ample strata of the Western middle class too. Then, there is no reason to believe that right-wing populist parties could not employ the neo-craft economic imaginary, tweaking its symbolic framework of reference towards more conservative instances of nostalgia (Gandini, 2020), leveraging on the traditional and the genuine to contrast a supposed antagonism to transnational corporations with the defence of national interests. For instance, the new far-right Italian government held by Giorgia Meloni seems to be pioneering such an attempt. It created a new 'Ministry of Food Sovereignty', appropriating the term from a long tradition of anti-capitalistic, leftist movements such as *via Campesina* and the World Social Forum. The new Ministry has the mandate to protect and support Italian local products against international competition. Furthermore, it renamed the Ministry of Business the 'Ministry of Business and Made in Italy', to symbolically highlight the priority given by the government to the protection and promotion of the traditional, typical and predominantly craft productions of the country. Relatedly, among the most significant measures announced in the field of education, there is the institution of the 'high school of the made in Italy', with the declared goal of educating Italian students to become expert craftspeople in the most iconic artisanal Italian productions, such as food, fashion, and design, among others. DeSoucey (2010) has analysed how typical, artisanal food and politics of authenticity shape and get shaped by nationalist sentiments. Craft products in general can be used for the same goal. After all, it is worth remembering that the artisans, independent retailers and small entrepreneurs that nowadays constitute the backbone of the hipster economy have been historically, in their quality of core members of the petite bourgeoisie, the electoral base of reference for the fascist regimes and for their epigones thereafter.

Lastly, it is worth considering one final factor, the concrete impact that will be measurable only in the long term, concerning the future of the concept of authenticity in a multipolar world. Indeed, as this book has extensively argued, the rise of authenticity is a phenomenon deeply entrenched in Western thought. It is impossible to conceive it without referring to the deep history of Western cultural schemes, intellectual figures, movements and harsh debates. However, today's world has proven Giovanni Arrighi's analysis of a gradual shift in global hegemony from West to East to be true. We live now in a world that is clearly assuming – or has already assumed – a multipolar physiognomy (and current international events seem to accelerate this tendency). This process has already caused a blending of entrepreneurial models and market economies (Arvidsson, 2019). The hipster economy is today a truly global phenomenon. Still, its global status is a legacy of the global cultural and economic declining hegemony of the United States, its manifestation in non-Western contexts being largely the result of a mixture of Western economic imperialism and cultural influence. The adaptation of the hipster economy to local cultures has for now largely followed the staples of glocalisation, like in the case of the owner of Bar Trench in Tokyo, embedding Japanese *shokunin* into the neo-craft economic imaginary, without challenging the clear-cut Western origin of it. A similar derivative nature can be inferred in cases such as the current quest for authenticity in Indian cuisine (Rana, 2022). However, it is arguably just a matter of time before the clinch of American cultural influence will become weak enough for more truly hybrid models of hipster economy to develop – or to be rejected altogether. With all probability, these models are already flourishing but remain invisible to the eyes of Western academia. In this context, it is of particular interest what could become of the meaning of authenticity, and how it could contaminate its meaning with other ones originating from diverse cultural traditions. I will refrain from adventuring in any observation on the relationship between the Western concept of the authentic self and potentially similar or equivalent concepts from elsewhere: I lack the knowledge to do so. But I hope that more competent scholars will pursue such a goal, developing postcolonial analyses and conceptualisations of authenticity, including their impact on artisanal economies (see, e.g., Zakrzewska, 2023). In a post-globalised world, it will be interesting to assess if these processes will have rebound effects, with South and East Asian alternative or hybrid formulations influencing the Western long-standing interpretation of authenticity as well. This could lead to significant developments, including the possibility of opening new paths for the re-politicisation of authenticity on a different basis from that of Western individualism.

Notes

Introduction: contextualising the hipster economy

1. I feel a preliminary clarification of my use of the term 'late modern capitalism' (or elsewhere 'contemporary capitalism') is needed. Unless otherwise specified, I will generally refer to the configuration of global capitalism in the context of Western or Global North societies. This delimitation must be understood as mere contextualisation: of course, I consider capitalism as a global phenomenon, as will emerge quite clearly in this chapter. I also believe that the decolonisation of thought begins by thinking on a global scale, all the while setting as a perimeter for the validity of our claims the contexts on which we have sufficient evidence and with which we are more familiar.
2. I mean this literally. The official report of one of these fundings listed as 'qualifying innovation' of one of the selected winners, the idea to fry *platanos* and sell them to customers.
3. Throughout the book, I will use micro-entrepreneurs to refer to the category of small business owners with none or few employees, typical of independent retailing.
4. 'Roach coaches' are, mainly in US slang, a way to refer to food trucks serving food with generally low hygiene standards at low prices. My interviewees in Italian did not use this term. They used the Italian term *lurido*, many times in one of its dialectal variants, which means 'scuzzy' and refers to the same type of food truck in its Italian version.
5. It is important to note that bars in Italy have distinctive features. Whereas cocktail bars usually open for after-work aperitifs, most 'bars' are in fact cafés, independent shops opening in the morning to serve coffee, cappuccino and croissants to workers, then sandwiches or simple meals during the lunch break, and which close in the late afternoon. They fulfil the role that in other countries is largely played by big chains and franchises.
6. Significantly, the Wikipedia entry about hipsters – at the time of writing this chapter – opens with the following sentence: 'The 21st-century hipster is a subculture (sometimes called hipsterism) that is defined by claims of authenticity and uniqueness yet, ironically, is notably lacking in authenticity and conforms to a collective style.'
7. Cultural *milieux*, as defined by Stuart Hall and Tony Jefferson (2006), are diffused and loosely bounded groups that express criticism of the dominant culture while remaining within its boundaries. They tend to characterise middle-class subcultures.
8. Michel Aglietta, whose book *A Theory of Capitalist Regulation* gave birth to the regulation theory school, defined it as an 'offshoot' of Braudel work (Aglietta, 2008). Arrighi was a professor at the Fernand Braudel Centre at Binghamton University.
9. They were actually not the first to propose this thesis. The new monopolistic nature of capitalism had already been recognised by Engels in the last decades of the nineteenth century and in further detail by Thorstein Veblen and Rudolf Hilferding at the beginning of the twentieth century, as well as by Lenin in his analysis of imperialism.
10. This notion can be easily validated by a quick mental overview of the number of companies that dominate each field of the digital economy: social networks, ride sharing, food delivery, short rentals, video streaming. Each of these fields is dominated by a handful of 'unicorns', with exceptions happening only for specific national markets or spin-offs saturating an unexplored market niche (e.g., a food delivery platform *specific* to food otherwise wasted).
11. Michel Aglietta expressed a similar opinion about the possibility of a prospective new Chinese regime of accumulation, in an article written for the *New Left Review* (Aglietta, 2008).

12. In accordance with the distinction (and opposition) between capitalism and market economy foundational to Braudel's interpretation of history.
13. See, for example, the Frankfurt School and Herbert Marcuse in particular, Henri Lefebvre, Jean-Paul Sartre, as well as Raymond Williams on culture, or Paulo Freire on education, as will be better illustrated in the next chapter.
14. In *A Theory of Capitalist Regulation*, Michel Aglietta discusses the Fordist 'regime of consumption', but following the Marxist principle of the primacy of production relations over consumption relations, this regime is reduced to a mere appendix functional to the regime of accumulation.

1 A *longue durée* quest towards the meaning of authenticity

1. At the moment, according to Google Scholar, the expression appears in the title of 177 academic articles or books.
2. See, for example, the excellent account of how craft brewers express authenticity by Thurnell-Read (2019), the analysis of authenticity in food consumption by Johnston and Baumann (2014), or the role of authenticity in urban transformations by Zukin (2010).
3. The list actually includes me, too, in my previous academic works on the topic.

2 The hip aesthetic regime of consumption

1. The idea of soviet countries fostering alienation as commodification may seem counterintuitive, but it is sufficient to think of Stakhanovism and the ideals of the virtuous man as the productive worker to get a sense of why younger generations could experience it.
2. I acknowledge a divergence from Bourdieu, in that I assume every individual has an aesthetic disposition, resulting from the interaction between aesthetic regimes and personal agency. Bourdieu, instead, believes that the presence of an aesthetic disposition is in itself a marker of distinction and inequality. He explicitly criticises a universalist approach granting the faculty of aesthetic judgement to everyone (and to the working class in particular) in *Pascalian Meditations* (Bourdieu, 1997) as a 'populist aestheticism' that is ultimately an illusion.
3. Despite their similarity, I use 'hegemonic' and 'paradigmatic' with different meanings. 'Hegemonic' – paying homage to the Gramscian theory of cultural hegemony – refers to the interpretation of an aesthetic disposition that becomes persuasive and pervasive in society to the point of being widely accepted by individuals as a matter of fact. A paradigmatic aesthetic regime of consumption refers instead to an aesthetic disposition that becomes distinctive and defining – from a qualitative, not necessarily quantitative point of view – of a capitalistic configuration.
4. Incidentally, Pascal's thought stresses even more the relevance of ideas of a condition of authenticity as opposed to alienation as far back as the seventeenth century.
5. During the months in which I have been writing this book, a global energy crisis and a spike in inflation are taking place due to the combined effects of the global Covid-19 pandemic and the Russian invasion of Ukraine, with dramatic increases in the cost of living. Furthermore, a growing number of experts consider it very likely that the start-up economy, fuelled by more than a decade of astronomical venture capital investments, may soon burst as a new financial bubble.
6. Most authors referenced in this section on the kitsch have been discovered thanks to the anthology edited by Belpoliti and Marrone (unfortunately, published only in Italian). To them goes all my gratitude for the impressive work.
7. Another focus of Peterson's research in the same years has been the rise of authenticity in consumption, but curiously the two theorisations rarely interacted in his analysis.
8. I am, fortunately, not the only one addressing similar goals. See, for example, Smith Maguire *et al.* (2022) for the theorisation of mobile trust regimes.

3 The renaissance of neo-craft industries

1. A partial exception to this rule could be considered digital makers, that can produce unique pieces at low costs thanks to 3D printing. Still, their production method can be considered artisan only in highly metaphorical ways.
2. A parallel can be drawn, again, with the back-to-land movement of the 1970s, when people abandoned the cities to go back to farming in the countryside. Neo-craft industries are also fuelled by a new similar wave.

4 The neo-craft micro-entrepreneurs

1. For more information on the doctoral dissertation and the followed methodology, it is freely accessible at https://air.unimi.it/handle/2434/708105 (last accessed 3 January 2023).
2. Even if multiple attempts happened during the years, see, for example, San Precario movement (Murgia, 2014).

5 The hipster economy and the urban space

1. The name is an acronym for 'North of Loreto', and a direct reference to 'SoHo' of Lower Manhattan, New York City.
2. According to the census, in 2011 57 per cent of the local population was Pakistani, 9 per cent Indian, and 5 per cent Bangladeshi (and the percentages are arguably higher now).

References

Adamson, G. (2018). *The Invention of Craft*. Bloomsbury Visual Arts.
Aglietta, M. (1979). *Theory of Capitalist Regulation: The US Experience*. New Left Books.
Aglietta, M. (2008). Into a New Growth Regime. *New Left Review, 54*, 61–74.
Alfoldy, S. (2018). Crafting Kindness. *Journal of Canadian Art History/Annales d'histoire de l'art Canadien, 39/40*(2/1), 178–85.
Amin, A. (ed.). (2011). *Post-Fordism: A Reader*. John Wiley & Sons.
Arrighi, G. (2007). *Adam Smith in Beijing*. Verso.
Arrighi, G. (2010). *The Long Twentieth Century*. Verso.
Arsel, Z., and Thompson, C. J. (2011). Demythologizing Consumption Practices: How Consumers Protect Their Field-Dependent Identity Investments from Devaluing Marketplace Myths. *Journal of Consumer Research, 37*(5), 791–806.
Arvidsson, A. (2006). *Brands Meaning and Value in Media Culture*. Routledge.
Arvidsson, A. (2019). *Changemakers: The Industrious Future of the Digital Economy*. Polity Press.
Bandinelli, C. (2019). *Social Entrepreneurship and Neoliberalism: Making Money While Doing Good*. Rowman & Littlefield Publishers.
Banks, M. (2017). *Creative Justice: Cultural Industries, Work and Inequality*. Rowman & Littlefield International.
Baran, P. A., and Sweezy, P. M. (1966). *Monopoly Capital*. Modern Reader Paperbacks.
Barbera, F., Cersosimo, D., and Rossi, A. D. (2022). *Contro i borghi. Il Belpaese che dimentica i paesi*. Donzelli.
Bardhi, F., and Eckhardt, G. M. (2017). Liquid Consumption. *Journal of Consumer Research, 44*(3), 582–97.
Barker, H., and Taylor, Y. (2007). *Faking It: The Quest for Authenticity in Popular Music*. W. W. Norton.
Baudrillard, J. (2016). *The Consumer Society: Myths and Structures*. SAGE Publications.
Beckert, J. (2016). *Imagined Futures: Fictional Expectations and Capitalist Dynamics*. Harvard University Press.
Bell, D. (1976). The Coming of the Post-industrial Society. *The Educational Forum, 40*(4), 574–9.
Belpoliti, M., and Marrone, G. (2020). *Kitsch*. Quodlibet.
Berman, M. (1972). *The Politics of Authenticity: Radical Individualism and the Emergence of Modern Society*. Atheneum.
Bologna, S. (2018). *The Rise of the European Self-employed Workforce*. Mimesis International.
Bologna, S. (2021, December 10). 'We can't leave the idea of freedom to the far right!' Angryworkers.org. Accessed 26 July 2023. https://www.angryworkers.org/2021/12/10/we-cant-leave-the-idea-of-freedom-to-the-far-right-sergio-bologna-on-the-green-pass/
Boltanski, L., and Chiapello, È. (2007). *The New Spirit of Capitalism*. Verso.
Bonini, T. (2014). *Hipster*. Doppiozero.
Bourdieu, P. (1984). *Distinction: A Social Critique of the Judgement of Taste*. Harvard University Press.
Bourdieu, P. (1997). *Pascalian Meditations*. Stanford University Press.
Bradshaw, A., and Scott, L. (2018). *Advertising Revolution: The Story of a Song, from Beatles Hit to Nike Slogan*. Repeater.
Braudel, F. (1977). *Afterthoughts on Material Civilization and Capitalism*. Johns Hopkins University Press.

Brewers Association. (6 December 2012). Craft vs. Crafty: A Statement from the Brewers Association. *Brewers Association*. Accessed 5 June 2023. https://www.brewersassociation.org/press-releases/craft-vs-crafty-a-statement-from-the-brewers-association/.

Brewers Association. (2022). Who We Are. *Brewers Association*. Accessed 5 June 2023. https://www.brewersassociation.org/who-we-are/.

Brockling, B. U. (2015). *The Entrepreneurial Self: Fabricating a New Type of Subject*. SAGE Publications.

Brooks, D. (2001). *Bobos in Paradise: The New Upper Class and How They Got There*. Simon & Schuster.

Brown, P. (2020). *Craft: An Argument: Why the Term 'Craft Beer' is Completely Undefinable, Hopelessly Misunderstood and Absolutely Essential*. Storm Lantern Books.

Butler, J. (1997). *The Psychic Life of Power: Theories in Subjection*. Stanford University Press.

Campbell, P. C. (1987). *The Romantic Ethic and the Spirit of Modern Consumerism*. WritersPrintShop.

Chomsky, N., and Foucault, M. (2006). *The Chomsky-Foucault Debate: On Human Nature*. The New Press.

Colleoni, E., Illia, L., and Zyglidopoulos, S. (2021). Exploring How Publics Discursively Organize as Digital Collectives: The Use of Empty and Floating Signifiers as Organizing Devices in Social Media. *Journal of the Association for Consumer Research*, 6(4), 491–502.

Collinson, D. L. (2003). Identities and Insecurities: Selves at Work. *Organization*, 10(3), 527–47.

Cronin, J. M., McCarthy, M. B., and Collins, A. M. (2014). Covert Distinction: How Hipsters Practice Food-Based Resistance Strategies in the Production of Identity. *Consumption Markets & Culture*, 17(1), 2–28.

Crouch, C., and Pizzorno, A. (1978). *The Resurgence of Class Conflict in Western Europe Since 1968: vol. 1*. Palgrave Macmillan.

Currid-Halkett, E. (2017). *The Sum of Small Things: A Theory of the Aspirational Class*. Princeton University Press.

Davis, G. F., and Kim, S. (2015). Financialization of the Economy. *Annual Review of Sociology*, 41(1), 203–21.

de Beauvoir, S. (1976). *The Ethics of Ambiguity*. Philosophical Library/Open Road.

de Certeau, M. (2011). *The Practice of Everyday Life*. University of California Press.

DeSoucey, M. (2010). Gastronationalism: Food Traditions and Authenticity Politics in the European Union. *American Sociological Review*, 75(3), 432–55.

Drucker, P. F. (1969). *The Age of Discontinuity: Guidelines to Our Changing Society*. Butterworth-Heinemann.

Durkheim, E. (1897/1951). *Suicide*. Free Press.

Duttlinger, C. (2008). Imaginary Encounters: Walter Benjamin and the Aura of Photography. *Poetics Today*, 29(1), 79–101. Accessed 5 June 2023. https://doi.org/10.1215/03335372-2007-018.

Elias, N. (1935). The Kitsch Style and the Age of Kitsch. In J. Goudsblom and S. Mennell (eds), *The Norbert Elias Reader* (pp. 27–9). Blackwell.

Endrissat, N., Islam, G., and Noppeney, C. (2015). Enchanting Work: New Spirits of Service Work in an Organic Supermarket. *Organization Studies*, 36(11), 1555–76.

Ewen, S. (2001). *Captains Of Consciousness Advertising and the Social Roots of the Consumer Culture*. Basic Books.

Featherstone, M. (2007). *Consumer Culture and Postmodernism*. SAGE Publications.

Fisher, M. (2012). *Capitalist Realism: Is There No Alternative?* Zero Books.

Florida, R. (2002). *The Rise of the Creative Class*. Basic Books.

Frank, T. (1997). *The Conquest of Cool: Business Culture, Counterculture, and the Rise of Hip Consumerism*. University of Chicago Press.

Fraser, N. (2022). *Cannibal Capitalism: How our System is Devouring Democracy, Care, and the Planet – and What We Can Do About It*. Verso.

Freire, P. (1970). *Pedagogy of the Oppressed*. Continuum Intl Pub Group.

Fromm, E. (2011). *Escape from Freedom*. Ishi Press.

Gandini, A. (2020). *Zeitgeist Nostalgia: On Populism, Work and the Good Life*. Zero Books.

Gentili, D., and Pope, C. M. (2021). *The Age of Precarity: Endless Crisis as an Art of Government*. Verso Books.

Gerosa, A. (2021). Cosmopolitans of Regionalism: Dealers of Omnivorous Taste Under Italian Food Truck Economic Imaginary. *Consumption Markets & Culture*, 24(1), 30–53.

Gerosa, A. (2022). The Hidden Roots of the Creative Economy: A Critical History of the Concept Along the Twentieth Century. *International Journal of Cultural Policy*, *28*(2), 131–44.

Gerosa, A., and Tartari, M. (2021). The Bottom-up Place Branding of a Neighborhood: Analyzing a Case of Selective Empowerment. *Space and Culture*.

Gordon, D. (2009). *Segmented Work, Divided Workers: The Historical Transformation of Labor in the United States*. Cambridge University Press.

Graeber, D., and Wengrow, D. (2021). *The Dawn of Everything: A New History of Humanity*. Allen Lane.

Greenwood, R., and Scharfstein, D. (2013). The Growth of Finance. *The Journal of Economic Perspectives*, *27*(2), 3–28.

Greif, M., Ross, K., and Tortorici, D. (2010). *What was the Hipster? A Sociological Investigation*. n+1 Foundation.

Guerriero, M. (2019). *The Labor Share of Income around the World: Evidence from a Panel Dataset* (Issue 920). Asian Development Bank. Accessed 5 June 2023. https://www.adb.org/publications/labor-share-income-around-world-evidence-panel-dataset.

Häberlen, J. C., Keck-Szajbel, M., and Mahoney, K. (eds). (2019). *The Politics of Authenticity: Countercultures and Radical Movements across the Iron Curtain (1968–1989)*. Berghahn Books.

Hall, S., and Jefferson, T. (eds). (2006). *Resistance Through Rituals*. Routledge.

Harrison, B. (1998). *Lean and Mean: Why Large Corporations Will Continue to Dominate the Global Economy*. Guilford Press.

Harvey, D. (1989). *The Condition of Postmodernity: An Enquiry into the Origins of Cultural Change*. Blackwell.

Harvey, D. (2007). *A Brief History of Neoliberalism*. Oxford University Press.

Hidalgo, D. A. (2022). *Dance Music Spaces: Clubs, Clubbers, and DJs Navigating Authenticity, Branding, and Commercialism*. Lexington Books.

Hobsbawm, E., and Ranger, T. (1992). *The Invention of Tradition* (Reprint edition). Cambridge University Press.

Hoffower, H. (2019). Millennials Only Hold 3% of Total US Wealth, and that's a Shockingly Small Sliver of what Baby Boomers Had at their Age. *Business Insider*. Accessed 5 June 2023. https://www.businessinsider.com/millennials-less-wealth-net-worth-compared-to-boomers-2019-12.

Huxford, R. (1998). Urban Villages: An Introduction. Ice Briefing Sheet. *Proceedings of the Institution of Civil Engineers – Municipal Engineer*, *127*(4), 204–6.

Jayne, M., and Bell, D. (2017). *City of Quarters: Urban Villages in the Contemporary City*. Routledge.

Jesi, F. (2014). *Spartakus: The Symbology of Revolt*. Seagull Books.

Jessop, B. (2001). *Regulation Theory and the Crisis of Capitalism*. Edward Elgar Publishing.

Jessop, B. (2009). Cultural Political Economy. *Critical Policy Studies*, *3*(4), 336–56.

Johnston, J., and Baumann, S. (2014). *Foodies: Democracy and Distinction in the Gourmet Foodscape*. Routledge.

Juul, J. (2019). *Handmade Pixels: Independent Video Games and the Quest for Authenticity*. MIT Press.

Kinzey, J. (2012). *The Sacred and the Profane: An Investigation of Hipsters*. Zero Books.

Kulka, T. (1996). *Kitsch and Art* (1st edition). Pennsylvania State University Press.

Laclau, E. (2006). *Emancipation(s)* (p. 128). Verso Books.

Land, C. (19 November 2018). Back to the Future: Re-imagining Work through Craft. *Futures of Work*. Accessed 5 June 2023. https://futuresofwork.co.uk/2018/11/19/back-to-the-future-re-imagining-work-through-craft/.

Langlands, A. (2017). *Craeft: How Traditional Crafts are About More than Just Making* (1st edition). Faber and Faber.

Lash, S., and Urry, J. (1987). *The End of Organized Capitalism*. University of Wisconsin Press.

Lefebvre, H. (2014). *Critique of Everyday Life*. Verso.

Leslie, E. (2000). *Walter Benjamin: Overpowering Conformism*. Pluto Press.

Lizardo, O., and Skiles, S. (2012). Reconceptualizing and Theorizing 'Omnivorousness': Genetic and Relational Mechanisms. *Sociological Theory*, *30*(4), 263–82.

Lordon. (2014). *Willing Slaves of Capital: Spinoza and Marx on Desire* (Reprint edition). Verso.

Lowenthal, D. (1999). Authenticity: Rock of Faith or Quicksand Quagmire? *Conservation: The Getty Conservation Institute Newsletter*, *14*(3), 5–8.

Löwy, M. (1987). The Romantic and the Marxist Critique of Modern Civilization. *Theory and Society*, *16*(6), 891–904.

Lukes, S. (2006). *Individualism*. ECPR Press.

MacCannell, D. (1999). *The Tourist: A New Theory of the Leisure Class*. University of California Press.

MacDonald, D. (2011). *Masscult and Midcult: Essays Against the American Grain*. NYRB Classics.

Maly, I., and Varis, P. (2016). The 21st-Century Hipster: On Micro-Populations in Times of Superdiversity. *European Journal of Cultural Studies*, 19(6), 637–53.

Marchi, V. (2014). *Teppa: Storie del conflitto giovanile dal Rinascimento ai giorni nostri*. Red Star Press.

Marcuse, H. (1974). *Eros and Civilization: A Philosophical Inquiry into Freud*. Beacon Press.

Marx, K., and Engels, F. (1988). *The Economic and Philosophic Manuscripts of 1844 and the Communist Manifesto* (M. Milligan, trans.) (1st edition). Prometheus.

McWilliams, D. (2015). *The Flat White Economy: How the Digital Economy is Transforming London and Other Cities of the Future*. Gerald Duckworth & Co.

Merrifield, A. (2017). *The Amateur: The Pleasures of Doing What You Love*. Verso.

Mills, C. W. (1951). *White Collar: The American Middle Classes*. Oxford University Press.

Murgia, A. (2014). Representations of Precarity in Italy. *Journal of Cultural Economy*, 7(1), 48–63.

Neal, P. (2003). *Urban Villages and the Making of Communities*. Taylor & Francis.

Neff, G. (2013). *Venture Labor: Work and the Burden of Risk* (1st edition). MIT Press.

New America. (2019). *The Emerging Millennial Wealth Gap*. New America. Accessed 5 June 2023. http://newamerica.org/millennials/reports/emerging-millennial-wealth-gap/.

Ocejo, R. E. (2017). *Masters of Craft*. Princeton University Press.

Olalquiaga, C. (1998). *The Artificial Kingdom: A Treasury of the Kitsch Experience*. Pantheon Books.

Peach, A. (2013). What Goes Around Comes Around? Craft Revival, the 1970s and Today. *Craft Research*, 4(2), 161–79.

Peterson, R. A., and Kern, R. M. (1996). Changing Highbrow Taste: From Snob to Omnivore. *American Sociological Review*, 61(5), 900.

Pew Center. (2020). *Trends in U.S. Income and Wealth Inequality*. Pew Center. Accessed 5 June 2023. https://www.pewresearch.org/social-trends/2020/01/09/trends-in-income-and-wealth-inequality/.

Piketty, T. (2017). *Capital in the Twenty-First Century* (Reprint edition). Harvard University Press.

Piore, M., and Sabel, C. (1986). *The Second Industrial Divide: Possibilities for Prosperity* (Reprint edition). Basic Books.

Potter, A. (2011). *The Authenticity Hoax: Why the 'Real' Things We Seek Don't Make Us Happy* (Reprint edition). Harper Perennial.

Rana, N. K. (2022). The Perpetual Quest for 'Authenticity' in Indian Cuisine: An Answer through History and Folklore. *Digital: A Journal of Foodways and Culture*, 9(1).

Rhodes, C. (2021). *Woke Capitalism: How Corporate Morality is Sabotaging Democracy*. Bristol University Press.

Riesman, D., Glazer, N., Denney, R., and Gitlin, T. (1950). *The Lonely Crowd: A Study of the Changing American Character*. Yale University Press.

Rousseau, J.-J. (1817). *Emile* (vol. 2). A. Belin.

Salice, S. M., and Pais, I. (2017). Sharing Economy as an Urban Phenomenon: Examining Policies for Sharing Cities. In *Policy Implications of Virtual Work* (pp. 199–228). Springer.

Sartre, J.-P. (1957/2009). *Critique of Dialectical Reason*. Verso Books.

Schroeder, J. E. (2002). *Visual Consumption*. Routledge.

Scott, M. (2017). 'Hipster Capitalism' in the Age of Austerity? Polanyi Meets Bourdieu's New Petite Bourgeoisie. *Cultural Sociology*, 11(1), 60–76.

Seeman, M. (1975). Alienation Studies. *Annual Review of Sociology*, 1(1), 91–123.

Sennett, R. (2008). *The Craftsman*. Yale University Press.

Simmel, G. (1903/1961). The Metropolis and Mental Life. University of Chicago Press.

Simmel, G., and Hughes, E. C. (1949). The Sociology of Sociability. *American Journal of Sociology*, 55(3), 254–61.

Slater, D. (1997). *Consumer Culture and Modernity* (1st edition). Polity.

Smith Maguire, J. (2018a). Taste as Market Practice: The Example of 'Natural' Wine. *Consumer Culture Theory*, 19, 71–92.

Smith Maguire, J. (2018b). The Taste for the Particular: A Logic of Discernment in an Age of Omnivorousness. *Journal of Consumer Culture*, 18(1), 3–20.

Smith Maguire, J. (2019). Taste, Legitimacy, and the Organization of Consumption. In F. F. Wherry and I. Woodward (eds), *The Oxford Handbook of Consumption* (pp. 197–213). Oxford University Press.

Smith Maguire, J., Ocejo, R. E., and DeSoucey, M. (2022). Mobile Trust Regimes: Modes of Attachment in an Age of Banal Omnivorousness. *Journal of Consumer Culture*, 1–20.

Smith, W. R. (1956). Product Differentiation and Market Segmentation as Alternative Marketing Strategies. *Journal of Marketing*, *21*(1), 3–8.

Srnicek, N. (2016). *Platform Capitalism*. Polity Press.

Sum, N.-L. (2009). The Production of Hegemonic Policy Discourses: 'Competitiveness' as a Knowledge Brand and its (Re-)Contextualization. *Critical Policy Studies*, *3*(2), 184–203.

Sum, N.-L., and Jessop, B. (2013). *Towards a Cultural Political Economy: Putting Culture in its Place in Political Economy*. Edward Elgar Publishing Limited.

Thiel, P., and Masters, B. (2014). *Zero to One*. Crown Business.

Thornton, S. (1995). *Club Cultures: Music, Media and Subcultural Capital* (1st edition). Polity.

Thurnell-Read, T. (2019). A Thirst for the Authentic: Craft Drinks Producers and the Narration of Authenticity. *The British Journal of Sociology*, *70*(4), 1448–68.

Trilling, L. (1972). *Sincerity and Authenticity*. Harvard University Press.

Tronti, M., and Broder, D. (2019). *Workers and Capital* (D. Broder, trans.) (p. 400). Verso Books.

Turner, F. (2008). *From Counterculture to Cyberculture: Stewart Brand, the Whole Earth Network, and the Rise of Digital Utopianism*. University of Chicago Press.

Wallerstein, I. (2011). *Historical Capitalism with Capitalist Civilization* (3rd edition). Verso.

Warde, A., Wright, D., and Gayo-Cal, M. (2007). Understanding Cultural Omnivorousness: Or, the Myth of the Cultural Omnivore. *Cultural Sociology*, *1*(2), 143–64.

Webber, J. (2013). *The Existentialism of Jean-Paul Sartre*. Routledge.

Whyte, W. H. (1956). *The Organization Man*. Simon & Schuster.

Williams, R. (1976/2015). *Keywords: A Vocabulary of Culture and Society* (New edition). Oxford University Press.

Williams, R. (1977). *Culture and Society: 1780–1950*. Penguin Books.

Zakrzewska, B. B. (2023). *Anti-manual for the Organizational Construction of Authenticity in Postcolonial Contexts* [PhD, University of Sussex]. Accessed 5 June 2023. http://sro.sussex.ac.uk/id/eprint/110605/.

Zukin, S. (1982). *Loft - Living: Culture and Capital in Urban Change*. Johns Hopkins University Press.

Zukin, S. (2010). *Naked Cities: The Death and Life of Authentic Urban Places*. Oxford University Press.

Index

accumulation, regime of, 7, 39–41, 50, 56, 69, 117, 118
   Fordist, 7–8, 50–51 *see also* Fordism
   Post–Fordist, 9, 11, 45 *see also* post–Fordism
aesthetic disposition, 17, 39–41, 43, 98, 107–8, 118
aesthetic regime of consumption, 19, 28, 32, 37–39, 41–3, 71, 82, 101–3, 108–10, 113, 118
   hip, 46–51, 54–6, 62, 65, 69, 90, 94
   kitsch/pop, 50–7
aesthetics, 4, 27, 44, 47, 50–1, 53, 101
   legitimate, 46, 81
   middle–class, 57, 74
   and taste, 38–43 *see also* taste
alienation, 31–35, 37–38, 49, 99, 109–11, 118 *see also* authenticity and alienation
   in Romanticism, 21–27
   of salaried work, 76–7
   under Fordism, 12–13, 52, 55, 101 *see also* Fordism
Arrighi, Giovanni, 7, 9–10, 117
artisans, 3, 59, 61, 63–4, 79, 115, 119 *see also* craft
arts and crafts movement, 20, 26, 33, 109
Arvidsson, Adam, 10, 45, 49, 62, 77, 115
Asia, 3, 10, 53, 94, 103, 116
aura,
   authentic, 18, 21, 47, 54, 92, 102, 109, 111–12
   neo–craft, 54, 72 *see also* neo–craft
   pop, 50
   in Walter Benjamin, 72
authenticity,
   and alienation, 23–26, 31–35, 110
   and craft, 60–62
   and economic imaginaries of consumption, 71–4
   and hipsterism, 13–15
   and kitsch, 52–54
   and neo–craft entrepreneurs, 80–1, 83–4, 86–8, 90–1
   and the Romantic ethos, 20–4
   and the self, *see* self, authentic
   and urban space, 100–105
   as an atmosphere, 95–6
   definition of, 32–6
   existential 13, 25, 29–31
   in marketing, 45–7
   meaning of, 19, 29, 83, 115
   quest for, 20, 61
   relationships, 96, 111
   the future of, 110–17

Baudrillard, Jean, 39, 53
Benjamin, Walter, 21, 53, 72 *see also* aura in Walter Benjamin
Berman, Marshall, 23–5, 27, 37
Bologna, Sergio, 76, 114
Boltanski, Luc and Chiapello, Eve, 12–13, 46, 75 *see also* capitalism, new spirit of
Bourdieu, Pierre, 40, 42, 57, 118
Braudel, Fernand, 7, 20, 73

capitalism, 6–7, 12–15, 34–35, 85–6, 108–9, 111–12, 117–18
   competitive, 7, 31
   monopoly, 7–9, 19, 117
   neoliberal, 49, 112 *see also* neoliberalism
   new spirit of, 13–14, 22, 46
Chomsky, Noam, 29, 34
class, 41, 45, 54–7, 79, 90, 99
   middle class, 5–6, 11, 27, 34, 45, 48, 52, 55, 64, 68, 72, 90, 102–4, 108–9, 114
   working class, 37, 50–7, 61, 74, 90–1, 114, 118
commercialisation, 20, 24, 28, 34–6, 49, 111–12
   of social life, 26, 28, 34
   of subcultures, 47
commodification, 24, 28–30, 34–7, 72–3, 109, 118
   of authenticity, 86, 90, 111
   of the self, 29, 49, 72
   of social life, 28, 34
community, 66, 96–98, 103–4
countercultures, 5, 12, 14, 46–7, 67, 105
craft, 27, 33, 35, 48, 51, 54, 60, 71–2, 87–8 *see also* authenticity and craft
   beers, 17, 61, 63–4, 66–7
   craftwashing, 67
   as ephemeral objects, 63–5
   production, 65, 67, 83, 109, 114
crafty, 66–9, 72–3
   capitalism, 73, 78
cultural
   hegemony, 55–6, 70, 108, 118
   industries, 46–7
   intermediaries, *see* taste dealers
   omnivorousness, 54

cultural political economy, 69–70
   of taste, 55–6 *see also* taste
culture, 19–20, 27, 33, 50–1, 53, 55, 118
   mainstream, 6, 47 *see also* mainstream
   popular, 53, 55

de Beauvoir, Simone, 30–1
de Certeau, Michel, 87, 89
digital economy, 9–10, 77, 117
digital platforms, 1, 9, 53
distinction, 40–45, 51, 54–7, 68–9, 79–80, 118
distinctiveness, 18, 34–6, 45–7, 54, 65, 67, 80, 87, 100, 102–3

economic imaginary of consumption, 68–70, 86–7, 94
   authentic, *see* authenticity and economic imaginaries of consumption
   neo–craft, 70–3, 80–3, 87–91, 94, 96, 98, 101, 108–10, 114–15
Elias, Norbert, 50–1
entrepreneurial self, 75–8, 113
Europe, 7, 10, 12, 24, 26, 29, 37, 64, 76, 93

finance, 1, 8–11, 98, 100, 102, 118
floating signifiers, 86–7, 112
Florida, Richard, 99–101
food, 44–5, 59–65, 67–8, 73–4, 82–3, 90–1, 94–5, 114, 117
   and beverage, 1, 17, 45, 62–3, 65, 83
   trucks, 1, 4–5, 69, 75, 78, 80, 84, 117
Fordism, 7–8, 11–13, 31–2, 50–2, 55, 101, 109–10, 118
freedom, 29–32, 35–6, 45, 81–2, 85–6, 111
   and self–expression, 26, 76 *see also* self, expression
Freire, Paulo, 29, 34
Fromm, Erich, 29, 36

Gandini, Alessandro, 5, 11, 114
younger generations, 11, 18, 37, 103, 118
gentrification, 94, 101–2, 104
goods,
   external, 42, 82, 84, 87
   internal, 42, 81–2, 84
Graeber, David and Wengrow, David, 26
Gramsci, Antonio, 69, 108, 112, 118 *see also* cultural hegemony

Harvey, David, 8–9
hipsterism, vii, 13–14, 18, 19, 26, 60, 65, 68, 107–8, 117 *see also* authenticity and hipsterism
   as a subculture, 4–6, 12, 44, 68, 111
hipster
   economy, 4, 60, 81, 93–4, 98–104, 107–15
   label, 4–6, 108
   neighbourhoods, 93–4, 98, 100–3
   paradox, 5, 14
   urban economy, 102, 112–13
hipsters 4–6, 14, 60, 65, 68, 107–8, 117

individualism, 76–7, 79, 114, 116
industrial production, 20, 27, 62, 65, 88, 109

opposed to craft, 33, 35
industrialization, 20, 23–5, 30, 33–4, 51, 53, 60, 72, 109
industrious economy, 10, 49, 53, 77–9
Italy, 1, 3, 35, 48, 63–4, 73, 79, 114, 117–18
   Italian beer, 66
   Italian comedies, 52, 83
   Italian food, 90–1, 94

Jacobs, Jane, 85, 99, 101

kitsch, *see* authenticity and kitsch and kitsch/ pop aesthetic regime of consumption

Land, Chris, 27, 61, 63, 71
Lefebvre, Henri, 28–9, 35
longue durée, approach, 9, 20, 32–3, 38, 108, 110
Lordon, Frédéric, 85–6

mainstream, 6–7, 13–14, 28, 45, 47, 53, 107, 111
   alternative to, 5–6, 13, 50, 100
marketing, 22, 45–8, 51, 54–6, 62 *see also* authenticity in marketing
Marcuse, Herbert, 29, 34, 118
Marx, Karl, 7, 12, 22–3, 78, 85
   Marxism, 23, 28–32
mass consumption, 7, 12, 51
mass production, 7, 12, 38, 45, 51, 60, 62
massification, 6, 12, 33–7, 50
Merrifield, Andy, 85
Midnight Asia, 3, 103
Morris, William, 26–8, 35, 52, 63, 109

neo–craft 60–61, 67–73 *see also* economic imaginary of consumption, neo–craft
   economy, 59, 69–70, 73, 78, 89–90
   entrepreneurs, 17, 61, 69, 73, 77–91, 94–6, 98, 100, 104, 119 *see also* authenticity and neo–craft entrepreneurs
   entrepreneurial identity, 79–83
   industries, 59, 63–6, 74–5, 80–1, 84, 86, 90, 109
   renaissance of, 60, 62–3, 65
neoliberalism, 9, 11, 14, 48, 63, 75–6, 86, 113–14 *see also* post–Fordism
nostalgia, 11, 25, 52, 62, 114

Ocejo, Richard E., 2–3, 5, 71

passion, 61, 81, 82–86, 88, 96
petty conspicuous consumption, 65, 70
post–Fordism, 7–14, 28, 32, 46, 48, 53, 55, 61–63, 69, 75, 77, 84, 109, 111

regulation, mode of, 9, 38–41, 49, 56
   Fordist, 7, 13, 50, 51 *see also* Fordism
   neoliberal 9, 45, 48, 113 *see also* neoliberalism and post–Fordism
regulation school/theory, 7, 13, 38, 117
Romanticism, 21, 23–4, 26 *see also* authenticity and the Romantic Ethos
Rousseau, Jean–Jacques, 24–8, 33, 56
Ruskin, John, 26

Sartre, Jean–Paul, 30–1, 33–4, 75
self, 21–3, 33–4, 47, 49, 72, 76, 81, 103
   alienated, 21, 62
   authentic, 18, 24, 28, 34, 62, 95, 115
   entrepreneurial, 75–8, 80–1, 113
   inner, 23, 28, 35, 46, 85–7, 89
self–determination, 33, 36, 45, 47
self–employment, 8, 76–9, 84, 86
self–expression, 24, 26, 32, 45, 47, 62, 76, 81, 95
self–realisation, 37, 48, 81
sharing economy, 96–7, 99
Simmel, Georg, 25, 95
Smith Maguire, Jennifer, 39, 41, 43, 54, 118
sociability, 95–8
standardisation, 13, 19–20, 34–7, 44–5, 54, 88, 101, 109
start–up economy, 1, 9, 118
   entrepreneurs, 77–8
subcultures, 4–5, 13–14, 47, 107, 117
   see also hipsterism as a subculture and commercialisation of subcultures
Sweezy, Paul and Baran, Paul A., 7
symbolic capital, 42, 52, 55–7, 61, 65, 70–1, 77–8, 80–81, 94

taste, 17–18, 25, 38–43, 48, 53, 55–7, 73–5, 86–90, 108
   authentic 59, 90, 95, 109
   dealers, 41, 56, 75, 86–90, 104
   highbrow, 54–5
   lowbrow, 50, 54
   popular, 50, 60
technicised myths, 90–1, 98
Trilling, Lionel, 22–3

United Kingdom, 26, 59, 99
United States, 3, 6–8, 10–12, 20, 44, 50, 59–60, 64, 99, 115
   Afro–Americans, 6, 26
   native Americans, 26
urban village, logic of, 98–104

Williams, Raymond, 20, 23–4, 26–7, 33, 38, 40, 118
woke capitalism, 49, 78, 114
work, 3, 27, 40, 77, 79, 81–5, 98
   alienated, 35
   of art, 21
   artistic, 35, 84
   autonomous, *see* self–employment
   entrepreneurial, 61, 76–7
   experience, 75
   manual, 61
   meaningful, 62, 109
   passionate, *see* passion
   salaried, 76
   self–employed, *see* self–employment
   symbolic, 86, 104
workers, 3, 5, 12, 26, 51, 56, 63–4, 76, 85, 104, 117
   blue–collar, 14
   creative, 90, 100
   cultural, 93
   massified, 22
   passionate, *see* passion
   proletarian, 109
   self–employed, *see* self–employment
   sex, 19
   white–collar, 52

Zukin, Sharon, 46, 101–4, 118